Finlay J Macdonald, known to thousands of BBC radio listeners for his delightful 'Crowdie and Cream' talks, can look back on a long and successful career as a radio drama and talks producer, and as a television director. His *Journey to the Western Isles* retraces the steps of Johnson and Boswell 200 years ago, while *Crowdie and Cream*, *Crotal and White* and *The Corncrake and the Lysander* tell of his own childhood and adolescence in the Outer Hebrides. He now lives near Glasgow, working as a writer, editor and broadcaster.

FINLAY J MACDONALD

The Corncrake and
the Lysander

Futura

A *Futura* Book

Copyright © Finlay J Macdonald 1985

First published in Great Britain in 1985
by Macdonald & Co (Publishers) Ltd

This edition published in 1986
by Futura Publications, a Division of
Macdonald & Co (Publishers) Ltd
London & Sydney

ISBN 0 7088 2776 4

Printed and bound in Great Britain by
Collins, Glasgow

Futura Publications
A Division of
Macdonald & Co (Publishers) Ltd
Greater London House
Hampstead Road
London NW1 7QX

A BPCC plc Company

For Deirdre and Gillie

Chapter One

Not many people have seen an ox felled. But I have. And this is what happens. The would-be assassin stands two short paces to the side of his victim's head, and far enough forward to be able to look him straight in the nearest eye while he murmurs blandishments to the beast to reassure him and distract his attention from the long-handled fourteen-pound hammer which the man is dangling gently in the manner of a golfer addressing a ball. When the moment is right, and a degree of mutual confidence has been established, the man lifts the hammer to regulation hockey-stick height and then swings it forward with rhythmic force so that the business end of it makes contact square between the eyes. The ox jerks. For a split second he looks (not unsurprisingly) mildly surprised. And then he buckles at the knees and folds to the ground.

That was exactly how Old Hector reacted to my proposal except that he couldn't fall to the ground because he was sitting in a chair with arms on it – which is a different thing altogether from an armchair. But, unlike the ox, Hector recovered. And, very much unlike an ox, the blow was to prove the best thing that had ever happened to him in a life not, hitherto, crowded with good things.

Old Hector always described himself as 'an ex-mariner' although the one and only voyage of his youth had ended ignominiously in Singapore after a marathon night on the booze. Unsympathetic sailors (themselves hardened to the hazards of the East) used to hint that Hector wasn't telling the whole truth; they would make sly mutterings about there being 'black houses furth of the Outer Hebrides' and that some Chinese fellow had misunderstood Hector when he had asked for directions to the local Free Kirk. But the jokes had stopped long since and people had accepted that a couple of innocent pints had merely accelerated the onset of a severe bout of malaria, which had blighted the poor man's life and left him with a slightly shaky pair of legs and a very firm aversion to manual labour. For sure, for a few years after his premature retirement from the sea, he had worked for several seasons as a ghillie to wealthy English fishermen visiting the Big House, but that had only compounded his problems; he had ended up with rheumatism and a chronic twitch towards his cap whenever he met someone whom he considered to be above his own station in life. The former would have given him a valid reason for resisting permanent employment even if the 1930s hadn't come along; the latter had made him an easy victim for his sister Maggie, who considered herself above most people on the strength of having spent four summers as a chambermaid in a hotel in Oban. Matrimony had evaded her even in Oban, and so, when she deemed Hector's resistance to be at its lowest, she announced that she was going to sacrifice her hopes and her future to looking after him. And that, in all fairness, she did. She cooked his meals and patched his clothes; she worked their little patch of land on the moor's edge and milked the cow morning and night; she even carried home a daily creel of peat on her back every afternoon of every day, summer and winter. Hector spent his life pottering around doing humble little jobs about the house, carting the byre and feeding the hens; in the evenings he did the rounds of the village houses, yarning and drinking innumerable cups of tea – careful always to be back in his own home at whatever hour Maggie stipulated. On the rare occasion when he stepped out of line Maggie would exact fearful retribution by forgetting to buy his weekly quota of tobacco when she made her weekly visit to the Duchess's shop or kept her regular rendezvous with the grocery van. Hector not only smoked an evil-looking cutty-pipe but he also chewed nibbles of tobacco which he bit off a damp length of Bogey Roll he kept in his waistcoat pocket. He was so addicted to his daily dosage of nicotine that he had been known to smoke his waistcoat pocket during a period of enforced abstinence when Maggie's memory had conveniently forsaken her.

The way I have put it there makes Maggie sound a virago. She was. But it also makes Old Hector sound a pickthank – which he wasn't. It was just that he found it easier to float along on his sister's modest approval rather than face up to the tirades which he knew would be provoked by any self-assertion on his part. He was also very shrewd and he knew that a large part of the sympathy and good-will which he enjoyed among the villagers was a by-product of their attitude to Maggie, who was no more sparing of her tongue to them than she was to Hector.

But Maggie had died a long year ago, in the summer that the first aeroplane had landed in Harris. She had come home from the high moorlands with a sack of peat on her back and black thoughts in her heart for Hector, who was never to be found, by her way of it, when there was work to be done or peat to be ferried. She had dumped her burden at the end of the 'black house' as people called the crude thatched cottage out of which she and Hector had never moved, although the vast majority of people had forsaken those primitive dwellings for modern stone and lime houses or corrugated iron ones which, like our own, were supposed to be temporary till a 'white house' could be built. The black house, for all that it was primitive by advancing standards, was cosy; the fire sat in the middle of the beaten earthen floor and the smoke (or most of it) escaped through a hole situated obliquely above it so that any rain coming in didn't douse the fire beneath; the walls were seven feet thick, of dry stone build, and the only source of light was one small, deeply recessed, window. The combination of lingering smoke and limited light made for a gloomy interior in day time, but for a soft warm atmosphere when the lamp was lit at night.

But it was bright sunshine outside when Maggie huffed her way into the house that day, half expecting to find Hector sitting puffing his pipe now that the danger of having to go for the peat was over. She made her way into a darkness rendered blacker by the transition from sunshine to dim interior – and found herself confronted by a pair of large white eyes and a set of gleaming white teeth apparently suspended in nothingness three feet above the floor. It would have taken an imagination brisker by far than Maggie's to have puzzled out that a very dark-skinned Indian peddlar in a black suit was sitting on the fireside stool waiting patiently for her in the forlorn hope of selling her some items of finery from his bulky suitcase. But Maggie didn't even attempt to seek a rationalisation. She collapsed into a faint and Hector only discovered her when he fell on top of her, plunging his hand into the burning embers which Maggie had mercifully escaped. It was his yell of pain which had brought her back to consciousness but by the time they disentangled themselves the man whose name was not Mohammed had long since vanished from the village, presumably terrified lest he be arraigned in a foreign land for a capital crime.

We never found out who he was, or whether indeed he returned as one of the many Indian peddlars, who seemed to be discovering our village each summer, feeling safe in the camouflage of dark skin which made his kind look alike to us. Maggie lived for long enough to tell her story with superstitious enthusiasm and nobody had the heart to tell her the truth. What had happened was that the Indian peddlar in search of custom among the croft houses had bumped into one of the notorious pranksters of the village who had sent him climbing up the hill to Hector's house with the assurance that Maggie was desperate to buy a dress for a fictitious wedding. 'She's out at the peat,' said Sandy Cravat, who had earned his soubriquet from having acquired a certain amount of style during his seasons at the Tay salmon fishing. 'But she made me promise to be sure to tell you to go into the house and wait for her. Good luck, Mohammed –'

'I have told you, please, my name is not Mohammed –'

'Never you mind what your name is; just you go in and wait for Miss MacGeachan whose name is Maggie!'

None of that had come out, of course, till after poor Maggie had taken her stroke and died. Nobody ever thought of blaming anybody, even when the truth was told and her story of the teeth and eyes was, at last, believed. If there was blame at all it was directed at Sandy Cravat whose warped sense of humour had been the undoing of others ere then. Long after Sandy had settled into the sedating grip of matrimony there lingered on the legend he had created of the man of no name except 'the man whose name was not Mohammed'!

For the three days of Maggie's lying people had discovered nice things to say about her, in the way that people from Rome to Rodel find with the newly dead, but even then there were those who couldn't help putting a saw-edge on their sympathy. 'Poor woman,' they said. 'With that temper of hers it's a miracle that she didn't burst a blood vessel long since.' But the bizarre way of her final departure put an end even to the most veiled hints of criticism of her.

Her funeral was interrupted by no less an event than the landing on the beach of the first aeroplane, and those of the mourners who had the agility to match their curiosity had forsaken the grave-side to join the throng which had assembled on the beach to goggle at the silver De Havilland Rapide. Indeed one or two of them had taken advantage of the pilot's offer of 'a quick flip' before returning to consign Maggie to eternity. My father had been one of the curious and, although he didn't join in the free public relations rides, my mother's displeasure was no less vehement.

'A judgment will come on you people for your behaviour today. Mrs MacRae was in here and she'd been watching the whole thing from the Back of Scarista Hill. She said you looked for all the world like a stream of black cockroaches making for a dead sheep's carcase. It was easy to see that it was the missionary and not the minister conducting the funeral service, Mrs MacRae was saying, or he wouldn't have tolerated the gang of you rushing off to an aeroplane before poor Maggie MacGeachan's soul had been laid to rest. Mrs MacRae was horrified, and I'm not surprised!'

That was the point at which my father should have held his wheest. But he didn't.

'If God sends an aeroplane for Hetty MacRae's soul the way he did for Maggie's I'll be surprised!'

'John!'

And that was the last word before the long silence which lasted till early evening when, to the surprise of all of us, my mother went through to the bedroom and changed into her

11

Sunday frock. 'You two boys wash the dishes before you do anything else,' she said after she had made a cup of tea with more than the usual clatter of crockery. And then, without even looking at my father, 'And will you remember to milk the cow; I'm going out!'

'I didn't think you had taken to dressing in your finery for milking the cow. Although, mind you, she'd probably give an extra pint for seeing you looking as nice as that.'

She couldn't resist that, and I could see her twitching back a smile.

'That's what Hetty MacRae called in about. There's a sewing class in Drumpound tonight, and she doesn't like coming back alone past the cemetery after dark. Especially on an evening when there's been a funeral.'

'And since when did you start feeling so joco about coming past the churchyard at night?'

'We'll be all right with the two of us there – and there's a moon.'

'Ach well, you always got on quite well with Maggie, and she and Hetty haven't spoken to each other for two years so I doubt whether they'll start tonight.'

Her lips tightened again, but she decided not to rise to the bait.

'You be sure the baby's given a plate of semolina before he goes to sleep, and make sure he's dry.'

I was sent up the hill to bring the cow home as soon as mother and Mrs MacRae had set off for their sewing bee. It was only Spotty who was in milk; Rosie, having seen us through the winter, had now begun to go dry and soon the bull would be taking an interest in her. I found them both up at the little burn that separated the moorland pasture from the mountain grazing and they ambled gently down the slope in front of me – Spotty with her udder swinging heavily as she headed for the paddock gate. It was only in the last week or so that the township had started leaving the milking cows out on the moors overnight, and they still hadn't got into the rhythm of making their own ways home for milking. Soon they would arrive at the paddock gate precisely at eight o'clock – so punctually that you could set your watch to time by them.

When father came home with the milk pail, and after he had

strained and set the milk in its basins to cream, he settled down with a newspaper. He lit his pipe and propped his feet against the tall cupboard which served as dishes press, food store and pantry, taking up a substantial proportion of a living room which had been small enough for four but was, by now, getting claustrophobic since the new baby had brought the family up to five. While he had been at the milking I had embarked on an essay which the teacher had set us on the subject of the first landing of the aeroplane, and I was determined to finish it without help from him if I could. If ever I did invoke his help with an essay it brought out the frustrated writer in him, and once he got his teeth into a subject he took over completely even if it meant that the work on the croft or the loom went hang: invariably I had to spend more time rewriting and simplifying his compositions, in order to conceal their true authorship from the teacher, than it would have taken me if I'd written the whole thing from the beginning myself. But the subject of the aeroplane and its possible implications for the future of the community was proving more complex than I had thought and, in the end, I had to turn to him for assistance. His eyes lit up and he swung his feet down from the cupboard, but before he could get his pipe going to his satisfaction a knock came to the door, and he went to answer it with a puzzled look on his face; people didn't knock on doors in our village, they normally just walked in, and a knock at night-time usually suggested a stranger or a crisis of some kind. I was totally mystified when I heard our next-door-neighbour's voice talking urgently and so quietly that I couldn't make out what he was saying. I could hear expressions of concern and dismay from my father, and his face was white and strained when he came back for his cap.

'I'm afraid you'll have to finish your composition on your own, my boy. And remember to feed and change the baby. If your mother comes back before I do, just tell her I've had to go out and that I won't be long.' My instinct told me it would be unwise to question him and so, with my hope of an interesting 'new angle' having vanished I licked my pencil and got down to writing my essay on my own. By good grace I had just finished it when the door opened and my mother and Hetty MacRae burst in, clinging to each other and ashen faced.

'Where's your father?'

'He's out. Why? What's wrong?'

It was Hetty MacRae who answered, with her voice quivering and her eyes popping.

'Evil. That's what's wrong. I knew evil would come of this day when I saw men rushing from the blessed churchyard to view the devil's contraption on the beach. There are men digging in the cemetery. Digging! At dead of night. We didn't believe our eyes at first, but they're there all right. And I could swear it's Maggie MacGeachan's new grave they're at. What men of evil can't let the poor woman rest in peace? I wish your father would hurry up; I daren't walk home alone ...'

It wasn't in fact long before my father did arrive, and I could see that he was patently reluctant to talk in front of me. But he realised he had no option when he saw me staring at his boots. It was a tragi-comical story looked at from the vantage point of later years. A simple story – although it was serious of its time among people in whom religion and superstition were still fudging each other's lines of demarcation. Somebody fastened the coffin lid who shouldn't have done, and the result was that when Old Hector MacGeachan got home at last, having been fed by some kindly neighbour, but wearied and dispirited after the ordeals of the funeral service and the burial, he found Maggie still lying in bed; and he was too spent to take comfort from the fact that her jaw was firmly bound.

What was a simple community to do? There was no undertaker, no policeman, and certainly no Home Secretary in our new village, and so they took the only sensible course; they quietly dug up the empty coffin at dead of night and made sure that Maggie was in when they buried it again. They also made very sure that no murmur of the story got abroad, because the newspapers would have revelled in yet another story that smacked of 'Hielandism' and 'teuchterism'.

And so, Maggie had finally been laid to rest. She hadn't lived to see another man whose name *was* Mohammed take up his place as a respected member of our island community; she hadn't seen the village taking its greatest strides forward as the breakdown of the barriers separating the Hebrides from the mainland accelerated, and a weekly air service developed with the silver Rapide fluttering between mainland airports and our beach, providing fast if not comfortable travel for those who could afford it and a life-line in time of medical emergency; she hadn't seen the growth of a twice-daily bus service linking us to Stornoway; she hadn't seen the slow acceptance of the wireless by the few who could afford one of the ornate walnut sets requiring a dry battery and an accumulator to give them voice; and she hadn't heard the insidious influx of English words that radio was beginning to feed into our native Gaelic. She probably wouldn't have been impressed anyway because she professed a disdain for all new-fangled things, dismissing them with a sniff and claiming that she had 'seen all that sort of thing in Oban'.

After her death the village had rallied round Old Hector: the men had cut his peat for him and planted his potatoes; the women had taken it in turn to do his shopping for him with the result that he was never again driven to smoking his waistcoat, and they had taken it in turn to milk his cow for him morning and evening. In short, Maggie's death had been the beginning of life for Hector and it hadn't taken him long to wipe away the last obligatory tear.

The memory of those events of last year were idling through my mind as I made my way up the path past the graveyard in which Maggie slept, and I tried to push them away so that I could frame the words in which I would deliver my ultimatum.

In some mysterious way the job of milking Hector's cow had devolved on me since that day in May when I had sat the County Council Bursary examination for the second time. I had sat it knowing it was my last chance, and in the full knowledge that without the annual grant which was the reward of success there was no hope that my parents could afford to send me on to High School. Without the bursary I would leave school at fourteen and take a job as a roadman or a weaver or a jobster of some kind till such time as I might win away to the mainland to become something sophisticated like a commercial traveller. It had been drummed into me that there was no alternative to 'going away'; to remain in my own community, false prophets were assuring my young generation, was to be a failure. But at the beginning of July I had heard that I had won the coveted bursary and I would soon be leaving the village to embark on the first stages of that glittering higher education which would mould me for whatever future lay ahead. I had no idea what that future would be. Only dreams and fancies. I had been to the tailor in the Northlands and had been measured for a jacket; my first pairs of long trousers had been ordered from one of the Manchester mail order stores; a pair of 'Lornes' had been ordered from Northampton instead of the traditional winter boots. In three weeks' time I'd be boarding the blue bus, having left my home-spun, home-sewn image behind; I'd be leaving my brothers and Gillespie and the small world of friends in which I had been cosy and cocooned and in which the hard years of the thirties had been happy although, almost half a century later, I was to learn to talk of them glibly as 'bad'.

It was only when I put my foot on a thistle and stood, stork-like, on one leg to remove the thorns from a naked sole that I realised that I had been day-dreaming and had forgotten to frame the form of the words with which I would put my scheme to the old man whom I could see leaning against the dry-stane lintel of his doorway, puffing at his cutty, and waiting hopefully for any tidbits of news I might have collected for him. He'd been suffering from a summer cold and he had been keeping to the house, fearful of an onset of one of his occasional malarial bouts.

'Here you are at last,' he said as I reached him. 'I thought you were never going to come. Was that a thorn you got in your bare foot? Never mind, this will be your last barefoot summer; it'll be shoes for you all the year round now that you're going off to the High School like a posh young gentleman. Are you coming in for a puff before you do the milking?' He prattled on – his impatience at my late arrival already dissolved. 'Here you are. Five Woodbines I got Calum the Post to bring me, pretending they were for myself. It'll be a hell of a row I'll be getting from your mother if she spots that I'm allowing you to smoke here on the q.t. – and it's bankrupt you'll be yourself if you go on paying three pence every time you want five of these things. Three pence! You could buy three inches of Bogey Roll for that and it would keep you going for a week –'

'Och Hector, you shouldn't have done that. But thank you

very much.' I pocketed the flimsy green packet and then, remembering that I would buckle it when I squatted to milk the cow, I transferred it from my trouser pocket into my sleeve. 'I won't come in just now. I'll just get the pail and milk Primrose before she becomes restless and wanders away. I'll come in for a smoke afterwards.'

One of the rewards for the moil of milking Hector's cow was that I could smoke in comfort in Hector's house. I had started sampling the occasional cigarette when I was ten, but there was little satisfaction and no kudos in skulking with a cigarette behind a dyke or down among the seashore rocks on the odd occasion when one of 'the bloods' (the swaggering lumps of advanced teenagers) slipped me a dout, or a seaman cousin home on leave gave me a couple of fags from his duty-free pack; and so I hadn't really become addicted to nicotine – only to the idea, and the feeling of sophistication. My parents would have flayed me alive if they had found out, and this was one vice which none of the village parents would condone or conceal. But Old Hector wasn't a parent, and he got some kind of simple pleasure out of being able to share a plot with a youngster once he had got used to the idea. 'Ach, you'll be all right here,' he would say, reaching for his own pipe. 'I'll light up myself and if anybody comes in they won't be able to smell the cigarettes through my thick black.' This was the first time that anybody had ever given me a full pack (albeit of five) and I knew perfectly well that the old man couldn't afford thruppence. It wasn't meant as payment or reward, but it was that and more; it was a gesture of friendship, and a luxury for himself to feel that there was one small thing he could do for a fellow being. I felt a glow of affection for him welling in me as I sat in the peace of the dusk with my head tucked into Primrose's flank with the two jets of milk converging into one steady stream in the middle of the froth in the pail. Three continuous months of milking had strengthened my wrists so that they didn't get sore any more, and normally I got a lot of satisfaction out of trying to refine the rhythm of my pull. Now I was subconsciously aware that I was in perfect tune with Primrose because I could hear the matching rhythm of her cud, but my mind was far from being at ease ...

'Man alive, that's quite a pailful!' he said, taking the handle in

17

both his rheumaticky hands. 'That cow's milking better this summer than she's ever done. You sit over there and light up. I'll set out the basins later on; I haven't skimmed the creamed ones yet, but I'll do it before I go to bed. At this rate I'll have enough salt butter to see me through the winter ...' He prattled on as I sat down and lit a Woodbine and watched him trimming and lighting his single wick paraffin lamp; although it was still lazy daylight outside, the deeply recessed window of the black house didn't let in enough to light the faraway wall far less Hector's face. But by the time he had the soft light from the paraffin lamp trimmed to his satisfaction and was seated behind his pipe in the glow of the peat fire the scene was fit for Rembrandt.

We chatted backwards and forwards, and for once he had more news than I had because he had been talking to Calum the Post, who had become a richer source of information than ever since he had become the possessor of a wireless set. We discussed the news of the world, then the news of the village, but, at last, I had to come to the point which was worrying me.

'Hector,' I said, nipping my cigarette and carefully pocketing the dout for another time, 'you will have to start milking your own cow soon.'

He didn't say anything for a minute or two, nor did his eyes leave the fire. But at last he removed his pipe and spat accurately into the middle of the flames.

'O aye,' he said. 'You're not telling me anything that comes as news to me. I knew that you had to win the bursary this year; and I knew that you could and would win it because you've got a good head on you ...' He paused, and I waited for his eyes to moisten as I knew they would. He could control his tear ducts in a way that would be worth money to a television actor. When they were neatly brimming he carried on. 'Ah well, that's the way of life. And I'm glad for your sake that you'll be getting on in the world. You just go off to High School in your good suit and your posh shoes, and nobody will wish you better than I do; nor will I ever let anybody say that you didn't do your best for me while you had time. There's no way I can be milking the cow – me with my bad legs – so I'll just face up to things and sell her, even although I can't expect to get much for her with prices the way they are –' He paused for a moment of effect

18

and rubbed one eye with the heel of his hand. 'This is what comes of being old and a widower.'

Mentally, to myself, I conceded the age bit because fifty-six did seem like a ripeness of years then; and people did refer to him as 'Old Hector' although, in retrospect, that was because he acted old and sported a struggle of black beard with a white tip to it as if he had dipped it accidentally into a basin of flour. I couldn't find words quickly enough to point out to him that the loss of a spinster sister did not confer on an elderly bachelor the status of widowhood, and I couldn't bring myself to be totally unsympathetic to his affliction and hint that a man's legs were of minimal importance in the milking process. I knew that the real truth of Hector's present dilemma was that he was scared stiff of his quiet old cow, who didn't know what horns were for; and I also knew that if he did sell Primrose the crofters would see to it that he was supplied with milk for the rest of his life. But a cow was a status symbol in a crofting community, and Hector needed all the status symbols he could get. I allowed all these thoughts to fleet past because I had worked out my plan and I was going to stick to it.

'You'll have to get a wife – and quickly!'

I didn't know whether he was going to spit out his cutty or swallow it. He did neither. He bit on the stem till his jaw muscles quivered. He then snatched it out of his mouth and spat wide.

'A wife!' he croaked at last. 'I've heard tell that education could turn a man's head but I didn't realise till this moment that it made a bloody idiot of him into the bargain. Even if I wanted a *woman* in this place where would I find one, far less one who would look at *me*? And what woman in her sane senses would come into a black house with an earthen floor when there are houses with slate roofs and linoleum springing up all over the place? You're mad, that's what you are. Education and cigarettes have driven out any sense that you may have been born with.' He licked his finger and thumb and picked a small burning ember of peat from the fire and popped it into his pipe. He glared at me before he began to puff. 'And what's more you're not very respectful to a frail old man who sins his soul to make it possible for you to smoke.'

I had foreseen all his arguments, and I knew that there was a certain validity in them; desperate women were in short supply

19

in our part of the island. But I had also worked out my next move, and I re-lit my cigarette stub to fortify myself.

'I'll tell you what, Hector; we'll advertise!'

That was when he did his imitation of the stunned ox.

His eyes widened first. Then his mouth – and he didn't even attempt to catch his cutty as it fell to the floor. He was sitting in his Taransay chair – a severe wooden frame, with a high slatted back and plain stout arm rests, which made a mild concession to comfort in the form of a plaited marram grass seat. He gripped the arms to steady himself.

'Advertise!' he mouthed. 'Advertise for a woman –'

'No. For a wife.'

He gobbled silently for a moment or two and then, in a burst of energy, picked up his pipe from the floor and pointed it at me like an upside-down pistol.

'Go!' he said. 'Go and take your fancy ideas home with you and don't come darkening my door again or I'll tell your mother you were smoking *cigarettes*.' He made the word sound positively evil.

I shrugged and set off down the hillside, but I hadn't gone two hundred yards when I heard a querulous voice shouting to me that the cow had to be milked in the morning. I paid no attention.

It had been a daft idea I admitted, grudgingly, to myself, and I should never have upset the old man with it. Certainly I had seen adverts like that from time to time in some of the magazines that friendly tourists occasionally sent my mother when they regained the safety of their cities, and on rare occasions similar pleas had appeared in the local paper but people had usually laughed at the latter and assumed them to be jokes. For a day or two I had, indeed, convinced myself that it might be the answer to Hector's dilemma but now, having seen his reaction, I realised that even as a joke it would have failed. I glanced nervously to my left as I passed the cemetery, half expecting to hear the sharp voice of Maggie upbraiding me from where she lay under one of the anonymous hummocks over which the nettles were creeping. A corncrake rasped and I nearly jumped out of my skin, but the faraway answering call restored reality and gave its peace back to the dusk. My father was just reaching for the Bible when I got in, preparing to read the mandatory psalm and chapter so that my mother could get to bed and he could go back to the *Daily Express*.

'How was Old Hector?'

'Fine. A bit quiet when I left.'

'The poor old soul,' said my mother, putting away yet another sock that was destined for my suitcase. 'He's bound to get a bit lonely up there in that dark house.'

'He's all right,' my father said, yawning as he always did before embarking on his reading. 'Maggie's not so very far away – and she's quiet now.'

'John! How can you talk like that with the Bible in your hand?'

He smiled and began to mumble his way through whichever psalm the Bible had fallen open at. By the time I had opened my eyes after his quick little prayer my conscience had cleared itself and my thoughts had turned again to the prospect of going to High School. But I wouldn't have slept so soundly if I'd known that Hector was still awake.

Next morning I was halfway through the milking when I became aware of him hovering around, carefully keeping away from both ends of Primrose. I was surprised because when I had found the clean empty milkpail sitting outside his door I had assumed it to be silent reproach; normally I went into the house and collected the pail and, as often as not, had to wash it myself in the burn on my way to the impatient cow. Not quite knowing how to handle the situation I merely mumbled something about another fine morning, and when he didn't respond I guessed that the night hadn't soothed him any. I paid no more attention to him and took a tantalisingly long time stripping the cow. When I had squeezed the last possible drop of milk into the pail I whipped the fetter-rope off her legs and made my way back to the house with Old Hector waddling along behind me in silence. It was only when I'd set out the milk in two large basins and filled a jug for his brose and his tea that he summoned up the courage to speak.

'I've got a cigarette here that I scrounged off the shepherd this morning pretending that I was out of tobacco. It's a Capstan. There's not much of a smoke in those wee Woodbines. Sit down and light up like a good lad.'

I sat down, puzzled as to why he was now making such

friendly overtures when he had been so upset – with perfectly good reason – a mere twelve hours before. He pulled out of his pocket the wadge of newspaper he always carried with him for spill, tore off a strip, twisted it with great deliberation, lit it and offered me a light before getting his own pipe going. He tamped it and sucked it till it was drawing to his satisfaction and then he looked at me with a new twinkle of confidence in his eyes.

'I haven't slept a wink all night, boy. At first I thought you were mocking me and I was angry; then I thought you were pulling my leg and I was annoyed at myself for not taking a joke; and then, dammity, I got round to thinking that if I was wanting a housekeeper like they do in the manse and the Big House I wouldn't think twice about advertising, would I? And after all it's a kind of a housekeeper I'm wanting – er – at first anyway.' He chuckled and leant over and poked me in the ribs. 'I know they all think I'm a bit soft in the head, and, for all I know, the malaria may have got me there as well as my legs; but I'll tell you this, my lad, the malaria didn't hit me everywhere!' He gave me another poke in the ribs that nearly pushed me off the low stool on which I was crouched and he fell back in the Taransay chair chortling his head off. For a moment I wondered if he could possibly have been drinking, but then as he began to concentrate on re-lighting his pipe I could see that his eyes had gone deadly serious. I hadn't said a word, but I felt my throat tightening as it began to dawn on me that I might be hoist with my own petard.

'You're not being serious, are you?'

'What are talking about, lad? Weren't you being serious last night?'

'Well – er – yes, in a way, but –'

'I should hope so. I don't mind a joke but I'd be annoyed if I thought I'd wasted a whole night thinking and then discovered you were pulling my leg after all.' He bellowed his cheeks a couple of times to keep his pipe going and then went on in a crisp, decisive manner of which I didn't ever think he was capable. 'You're a clever fellow and you know about those things. You would know how to put an advert in the *Gazette* so that nobody would know who it was from, wouldn't you?'

By chance I did know. For the last couple of years I'd been obsessed with the idea of getting a bicycle of my own even although I knew that my parents' resources hadn't yet recovered sufficiently for them to contemplate even a humble outlay such as a second-hand bicycle would represent. But I had toyed with the idea of testing the market and, feigning curiosity, I had found out from my father how one sent an advertisement (as short as possible) along with payment and one's name and address requesting the paper to withhold identification and allocate a Box Number. I had abandoned the whole idea when I discovered that I couldn't afford the advertisement far less the price of the most decrepit bicycle which, my friend Gillespie assured me, would be equivalent to a whole quarter's rent for the croft. And that was that. But the Gaelic proverb 'Keep a thing for seven years and you'll find a use for it' was proving itself once again. My accumulated, and hitherto useless, knowledge of the ways of the advertising world was now going to come in useful in a totally unexpected way. My qualms began to disappear and I warmed to the business of explaining the ins and outs of small ads to Old Hector.

'That buggers it!' he said, and it flashed across my mind that I had never heard him using the mildest of strong language before. 'If I've got to give my name and address the whole story will be winging from the Butt of Lewis to the Sound of Harris before they've even cashed my postal order, and that'll be quick enough!'

I assured him that the whole thing was as secret as the ballot box. 'All you need,' I said, with my confidence rapidly returning, 'is writing paper and an envelope, half-a-crown for a postal order and commission and a stamp.'

'Right,' he said, reaching under the Taransay chair where he must have concealed a writing pad and envelopes, 'here are the first two of those. You do the rest.' He looked at me slyly. 'It's a good job that boys who smoke cigarettes don't give away secrets.' I could sense blackmail without having it spelt out to me. I borrowed his tobacco knife to sharpen the stub of pencil that he produced from his waistcoat pocket and we moved over to the table at the window to begin the first of many drafts.

'Who's the postal order for?' the Duchess asked when I went to her shop, ostensibly for a half ounce of Bogey Roll for Old Hector. We didn't get the newspaper from her any more since

23

the driver of the daily bus had taken to flinging ordered copies out of his driving window at the croft-houses along his route.

'Old Hector,' I replied glibly. 'He's sending off for a bottle of linament for this rheumatism; it's a new kind that he saw advertised in *The Witness*.' He and I had rehearsed the lie so well that I could look her straight in the eye without blushing.

'Him and his linament,' she said as she thumped a stamp on the postal order. 'Tell him from me that Kruschen Salts is the latest thing for rheumatism; linament's out of date.'

The rest was easy. Calum the Post must have been surprised to find a stamped letter in the red pillar-box across the road from the schoolhouse because people usually just hailed him as he passed and handed him their letters with the appropriate sum of money to cover the postage. But if he ever associated the events that followed with an envelope carefully addressed in block capitals, he never let on.

Our letter must have been beautifully coincident with the paper's printings, because there, in the very next issue, was the result of our joint composition.

Retired seaman wants woman used to croft work with a view to matrumony. Reply Box 427

'May the good Lord look down on us,' said Old Hector, unable to conceal the tremor in his hands. '*Retired seaman*, sounds like a captain when you see it in proper print; all I ever was was a deckhand and that only for two months.' He smiled nervously as he folded the paper away. 'The only consolation is that only a halfwit would answer an advertisement like that.'

I couldn't quite see how he could glean consolation from that particular line of reasoning. But I was half inclined to agree with him. And, in the end, he turned out to be rather more than half right.

Chapter Two

August was a slow month in the village – a time suspended between two seasons; between the dying notes of the corncrake and the forlorn bleating of the orphaned lambs.

The corncrake came in May when the wild iris was tall enough for her to hide. In our parts the sandy-oat crop, from which the experts had not yet weaned the crofters, was too late and too thin to provide cover for the supreme camouflage expert of all the birds, and so she made her nest where the bracken ended and where the iris began, with the result that the brown remains of last year's foliage among this year's green made her well-nigh invisible when she was crouched on her nest, and her eggs totally indiscernible when she was away. I spent long hours of boyhood searching for her – stalking her croaks as she held rasping conversations with faraway echoes, and once I found her lying dead on her back, as I thought, with her pale green belly matched to the iris and her striped legs pointing upwards, but when I bent down to pick her up she was away through the flag like a shuttle through thread and when she hawked a few moments later there was a laugh in her throat.

'You shouldn't have disturbed her,' Old Aunt Rachel said when I told her. 'Don't you know that it's millions of crakes lying on their backs with their feet up that keep the sky in place? And it's the strain of it that's made their singing hoarse over the thousands of years. Only fools hunt the corncrake,' she went on. 'And those with little to do. But the wise man listens to her and holds back the Spring work till her first croak tells them that the frost is over for good; nor will he take his scythe from the rafters till her chorus is ended. It was the coming of the scythe that made her start taking to below the water for the winter, don't you know? And if you don't believe me keep your eye on the moor lochs during the spring and you might catch her coming out from under the water after her winter sleep with a white patch on her forehead from the cold.' She chortled. 'In any case your chances of seeing her then are as good as your ever seeing another one; already you've seen as many in your short life as I've seen in my long one!'

Great Aunt Rachel was a lady for whom my father had instilled in me the equal feelings of awe and affection with which he regarded her himself. She was his aunt on his mother's side. Her pedigree stretched back to the 1780s – to a man with a broken leg who had been found half dead in the ebb on the beach below the old village on the foundations of which our new village had been built. In thankfulness for his deliverance the man, whose name was MacKay, devoted himself to the service of the church and, in due course, had begotten the family known as the Clerics from whom my father had inherited the love of education which he was so intent on handing on to me. Aunt Rachel was, for her time, well educated and well read but she had a vivid imagination which, over the years, had led her to believe that the man who escaped the sea on our shore was a survivor of the Spanish Armada, despite a minor chronological discrepancy of two centuries. If anybody was ever bold enough to challenge her with the apparent flaw in her history she would merely sigh pityingly, close her eyes, rock gently in her chair and recall Holy Writ –

A thousand ages in Thy sight
Are like an evening gone …

To that there was rarely any reply. But although the whimsies of the centuries always tended to get mixed up with Great Aunt Rachel there was always a glisk of truth where one least suspected it, and to this day I like to believe that, away back in my ancestry, a Spaniard lurks somewhere. Perhaps one day I will stumble across the truth of him just as I stumbled, very recently, across the old Highland myth that the corncrake hibernated underwater in winter and emerged in spring with a white spot on her forehead from the cold. The corncrake – in the less glamorous ornithological truth – migrates to Africa; the Highland legend confused the corncrake with her relation, the water rail. Of such facts and fancies were Great Aunt Rachel's dogmas compounded.

But she was right about the elusiveness of the crake. I never saw one again. But their stridulations from light dusk to brief dark in the summer evenings of boyhood were to become as implanted in the memory as the sound of the sea itself. I'm told that an occasional one can still be heard from time to time, but it's many years since they were loud enough to make the preacher raise his voice at evening service. I know now that the coming of the fertiliser landry was the beginning of the end of the crake.

We had long since got used to vans. Calum the Post's had always been with us, but it was not till the new road had been given a fine coating of gravel that people who had to pay for their own tyres and springs began to challenge the Duchess's monopoly with grocery vans and a fish van. The former didn't last long because a combination of wear and tear and tick made their profits minimal and their overheads astronomical. But the fish van had no competition either from the Duchess or the unfishable seas of our coasts; the fact that he was a Lewisman gave the fishman an age-old incentive to screw the last ha'penny out of his less worldly-wise Harris neighbours, and, although he only charged a shilling for a cod whose tail swept the ground when you carried him along by the head, Montgomery (who never had a first name) made enough to keep him going from his fish and saucer-sized biscuits which were hard enough to have been salvaged from the Mary Celeste. It may have been Montgomery's success that prompted his fellow islander to undertake a venture as bizarre as any entrepreneurial enterprise since the Icelander who sold the Aurora Borealis to the Edinburgh man.

Shortfield was a businessman who had crossed the Minch to live in Stornoway, but in all other respects he was reckoned to be sane. Till he conceived the idea of establishing a mobile

27

laundry service – in the shape of a large van which was scheduled to leave Stornoway on a Monday morning, travel down the west coast to Harris and back up the east coast, stopping at each croft house and picking up dirty washing which would, in two days' time, be returned crisply laundered to the grateful owners who would pay for it and replace it with more soiled linen destined for the same treatment. There was nothing wrong with the theory. Sitting in a warm office in Stornoway it seemed no more than reasonable to assume that harassed Harris housewives with large families, living in weather conditions where the most reasonable certainty was rain, would jump at the idea of ridding themselves of their washtubs, their scrubbing boards and their smoothing irons forever. Having, presumably, satisfied himself as to the cost-effectiveness of his dream, Shortfield (whose greatest asset was that he had an Old Testament first name) invested in a sizeable green van and a Lewis driver of inestimable charm and set them on the road to what he was convinced would be his fortune. Thus it was that on a Monday morning which I remember well, there appeared over the Back of Scarista Hill the laundry van which was to be known henceforth in the local dialect as 'the landry'.

But poor Shortfield overlooked three problems, and the third of them was probably the most insurmountable. First of all in those days very few women in Harris could contemplate the cost of sending their duddies away to be washed; in the second place not many of them had enough shifts to be able to send one set flittering off to Stornoway, and, thirdly and most certainly not one of them would be prepared to send her flannelette bloomers (far less her old man's long johns) to be held up and joked about by some lipsticked hussy in Stornoway. And so it was that, week after week, twice a week, the landry chuntered round its hundred mile circular route collecting nary a stich save, perhaps, an occasional linen table-cloth from one of the several manses and the few toff houses on its way. But the driver became a mini-celebrity. He was young and good-looking and cheerful, and so he endeared himself to blushing crofterettes and matrons alike; he always had some morsel of news from the burgeoning metropolis of Stornoway and so the men enjoyed his visits. But, more importantly, he was as obliging as Calum the Post and had all the time in the world to indulge in errandry, and so every time he returned to Stornoway he had a couple of his master's laundry labels full of orders for the chemist, the ironmonger, and the newly-opened Woolworth's Sixpenny Store. En route – because of the size and the emptiness of the van – he was able to carry much more in the way of heavy goods than Calum could carry; he could take half a dozen bags of peat, a couple of sacks of grain, several gallons of paraffin and a couple of newborn calves, without his van even looking low on its springs. Unlike Calum he was breaking no Government law; like Calum he was defrauding nobody since he was charging no fee for the services of a vehicle belonging to a master who was not in that form of transport business anyway. The landry took no time at all to become a valued institution.

Shortfield had the patience of the race from which he must have, sometime, inherited the name of Isaac; but he had none of that race's legendary business acumen. It can't have taken him long to realise that the laundry service wasn't making a profit; it took him a couple of months to accept that it never would. But, finally, he prepared to end something which anybody in his full senses would never have started.

But it wasn't as easy as that. The crofters had begun to like the idea of amenity. Calum the Post's van had paved the way for public transport in the shape of the twice daily bus; the various grocery vans (short-lived though some them were) had whetted the appetite for convenience; the fishman's van had proved a marvellous boon. But the landry had proved the greatest convenience of all – and here it was, suddenly, being withdrawn. There was uproar. Somebody wrote a letter to the local paper denouncing Shortfield for Tory, and repressive, and anti-social and all sorts of things; but the writer was careful to refer to the landry as 'the laundry service'. Poor Shortfield replied, claiming a white conscience and a red bank balance. But to no avail. The next letter was signed by the Clerks of half a dozen Grazings Committees trying to prove that a laundry service had become a social asset, and that by the very act of having instituted it the proprietor was under a moral if not legal obligation to keep it going, in much the same way as a landlord who concedes right of way is obliged to observe it forevermore ...

Of course it didn't work! No enterprise, even as private as Shortfield's, can be forced to go on making a loss in a public weal for which there is no public purse, and, suddenly, the laundry service was, as they say nowadays, axed. The jeremiad was brief, because crofters are resilient by nature, but what did remain was a new word. The word *landry* had entered the local Gaelic vocabulary as the generic term for a vehicle which carried for free goods other than those for which it was commercially intended. Thus, when the Scottish Co-operative Wholesale Society launched a mobile grocery service, with a spacious van and an obliging driver, the vehicle became known as the *Co-op Landry;* when the Post Office decided to overhaul the telephone system and gave its engineers a big green pantechnicon with room to spare it became, inevitably, the *Telephone Landry;* and when the Department of Agriculture decided to upgrade the traditional and fairly primitive agricultural methods of the new villages, the lorry which they sent round at regular intervals with fertilisers and new-fangled weed-killers became the *Fertiliser Landry.* And all of them provided supplementary free services which ensured that no professional road haulier need ever contemplate profitable venturing into the Southlands of Harris.

It was the Fertiliser Landry which began to put the seal on the fate of the corncrake as the hitherto fallow fields began to be put under ryegrass for early harvesting and as the boundaries of the bracken and the wild iris began to be pushed back and farther back. But the process was only beginning as my days in the village were ending; and during the whole of that August before High School the crake was in chorus still.

Perhaps it was a pity that it was too early in the afternoon for the corncrake to have raised her voice when the people from the six parishes assembled in our village to celebrate the first ever pastoral visit to our corner of the Hebrides of The Right Reverend, The Moderator of the General Assembly of the Church of Scotland – whose very title, to this day, is his protection against the sort of sexual assault which the literati of the lavatories invoke against the Pope. The Moderatorship is the highest honour that the Church of Scotland can confer on any of her servants but, unlike the Pope, the Moderator's term

30

of office is one year only – his appointment lasting from one month of May till the next. Like the Pontiff he is larded with pomp and ceremony and, nowadays, is expected to undertake ceremonial tours all over the world, blessing the poor and the benighted; kissing innocent babies; and chiding errant rulers for their misdeeds, having partaken of their hospitality. Nowadays every Moderator is expected to jet to foreign parts like a born-again American trouble-shooter; in those days before the war our new village (although not quite so new by then) probably qualified as an 'emerging state' and – having been without a pastor of our own for a few years – we almost certainly were deemed to be in need of rehabilitation and blessing.

The news of the impending visitation had been received early on in the summer and had been greeted with great excitement by the womenfolk, who hadn't even had a wedding to stir up excitement for the last long while. It was immediately foreseen as an occasion for new hats and outfits; a few mail orders were dispatched by the older ladies, but the younger ones had, by now, got into the way of taking advantage of the daily return bus journey to Stornoway to plunder the emporia of fashion which were laying tentative foundations in the town. Some of the less secretive wives organised 'excursions' and hired one of our own Southland buses for a day-trip which would include a visit to the Picture House. The men were less enthusiastic. 'Sure as bloody hell he'll come on the finest day of August,' somebody said. 'The day that the Grazing Committee will have set aside for the lifting of the lambs.' And his prophecy was to prove true.

We had been selected as the focal point for the Moderatorial visitation because the new village had grown up round the huge church which, for more than two centuries, had been Harris Church – the Protestant ecclesiastical centre of the island from the days when the arable rolling Southlands had been the only really populated part of the island. The balance of population had swung during the eighteenth and nineteenth centuries when the population had been evicted overseas to Canada, or to the rocky coasts of the north and east which couldn't be exploited for sheepfarming. Slowly the Northlands in particular had evolved a different way of life, based on fishing

31

and weaving. Round the magnificent anchorage of East Loch Tarbert a large village had been gouged out of the rocky hillside and it had matured into the administrative capital of the island with a dozen shops, a sizeable bank, a High School and the sundry other appurtenances of local government. Tarbert had two churches of different denominations, one of which belonged to the Church of Scotland and was thronged and active, but ours was still the traditional Parish Church even although a mere twenty people shuffled into its cavernous depths on the average Sunday. Tradition is cherished as much in the heart of the West Highlander as it is in the most aged institutions of the realm and the Harris Church had to be the scene of Moderator's pageant even although the organisation of it would be as inconvenient as would be the staging of the Coronation in a country village in Dorset.

Those who thought that the visit would be a matter of 'Hello' and 'God Bless' were quickly disillusioned. For that one day our tiny village was to be a centre of pilgrimage for a substantial hunk of the four thousand population of the island, and it was obvious that even the most dyed-in-the-wool fundamentalists from the other churches could not refrain from coming to watch the Church of Scotlanders worshipping their golden images and frolicking their way to perdition. By now it was common knowledge that, for this official visit, the Moderator would be costumed in the tricorn hat, lace ruffles, knee-breeches and silver buckled shoon of his office – the type of frivolity which would doubtless be preached against for weeks to come in the pulpits of the Free Church and the Free Presbyterian Church, both of whom held the Established Church as being only one step away from Rome and two from Hell. Nevertheless, come the day, the most ardent adherents of those creeds would undoubtedly turn out for the entertainment and would, if necessary, purge the sin of curiosity in some way later. Meantime, not only did they unobtrusively prepare to bedeck themselves suitably for the occasion but they contributed generously in cash and in kind to the preparations for the great day.

The Moderator was coming in a year when it was being borne home to people that the grim days of the slump and depression were really over. Incomes from all sources had

32

increased. The price of sheep and cattle had improved, and no longer was it more economical for crofters to kill off their newborn calves than to rear them for sale. Roadworks were being re-started in various parts of the island and tarmacadam surfaces were being laid on the busier roads of the Northlands around Tarbert. Fishing was becoming profitable again although that didn't concern us in the Southlands. But what did concern us very much was that tweed was once more in great demand at good prices; in fact ten times as much Harris Tweed was being produced in the Hebrides as had been produced in the lean years of the early thirties and, in our village, there was a loom in almost every home. My own father had stuck to his policy of concentrating on short lengths and suit-lengths for the network of customers he had built up from the ever-increasing flow of tourists; mother was able to buy occasional luxuries from the grocery vans now, but she kept on the job of school cleaner which she had been glad to get when money had been desperately tight and poverty had been our nearest neighbour. It was as school cleaner that she had to fulfil a role in preparation for the visit. It had long since become obvious that the hospitality of the village could not possibly cope with the sudden surge of gawpers, and since it was tempting Providence to bank on another multiplication of loaves and fishes even in the presence of the titular head of the Church of Scotland, it was decided to turn the schoolroom and schoolhouse into a temporary canteen. On and off since the beginning of July my mother and the women of the village had scrubbed and polished and planned, and when the Moderator did finally arrive they were handsomely rewarded with praise for their efforts.

The women managed to organise their part of the celebration with surprisingly little fuss and no formality. But the men kept organising themselves into committees which held endless and sociable meetings in different houses, but they had to keep re-forming themselves and appointing new chairmen when they fell out on some point or other. One of the main problems was that none of the men considered themselves good enough to be full members of the church (or communicants) and so they couldn't be office bearers. We therefore had the paradoxical situation of a Parish Church without minister or elders, and it wasn't always convenient for elders from neighbouring congregations to travel to haphazardly arranged committee meetings. Murdo Mor was by way of being a professional committee chairman by dint of his enthusiasm for public speaking and by virtue of his having acquired a knowledge of procedures of all kinds while he was some kind of salesman in Manchester; he was also an elder – but, unfortunately, of a small church which had long since broken off diplomatic relations with the Church of Scotland as a result of a deep theological disagreement as to whether Jonah had been swallowed by a Blue Whale or a White Whale. But Murdo Mor was a conscientious pillar of the community and he agreed to lend his experience and his gifts of organisation to ensuring the success of the social side of the great event, provided he wasn't expected to perform any duties that could be determined 'religious'.

Under Murdo Mor's chairmanship the 'steering committee' had performed remarkable feats of fund-raising, and it was known that at least a hundred pounds had been collected by the beginning of July for the purposes of organising transport for the old and the decrepit, for the printing of leaflets giving the orders of procedure and of service, and for the dozens of other things which required hard cash rather than volunteer labour. Yet he himself caused the first splintering of the co-operative spirit when he suggested hiring two marquees for use as public toilets. That was too much like posh for some people who hadn't themselves aspired as yet to interior plumbing in their own homes and, in the heat of debate, somebody was heard to say that if the Moderator couldn't organise himself sufficiently to have a shit before he left his Stornoway hotel then it was no wonder that the Church of Scotland was in constant schism. Murdo didn't hold any brief for the Church of Scotland but his years in Manchester had inculcated in him a certain delicacy where references to the bowel were concerned, and he promptly resigned his chairmanship for the first of many times. In the end, the matter of comfort was resolved when somebody remembered that the County Council had spent a large sum of money installing dry closets in the school playground (conveniences which the pupils had disdained for two years) and a small sum of money was set aside for their rehabilitation, and an amiable lad called 'Daft Jimmie' from Drumpound was given five shillings to paint appropriate signs – but principally to keep him out of mischief.

Although I hadn't realised it, the pastoral visit had been scheduled fifteen months before – as soon as it was known that the Moderator Designate was a Gaelic speaker – and the staff at the Head Office of the Church of Scotland in Edinburgh had been quietly organising things with the sort of practised ease that the Lord Chamberlain's office brings to functions of Royal life and death. Unfortunately they didn't consider it necessary to keep the local community fully informed, and, consequently much duplicated effort led to occasional embarrassment. At least two ministers had spent their summer weeks preparing welcoming addresses – at the invitation of two separate parish committees – while the man who was eventually to deliver it had been, in fact, appointed by the Presbytery months before. It was only by the grace of God that three Divines weren't jostling for the pulpit when the day came.

'Mark my words,' Old Hector had said to me the day after I had posted the letter with his advertisement to the *Gazette*. 'There will be such a stramash here for the next three weeks that we could be putting a notice in the school window advertising for a wife and nobody would be noticing it.' He had been trying to bolster his own flagging confidence, but he wasn't far wrong. *Moderator fever* was beginning to grip the village and the most pious were not always the ones who were enjoying it most. Apart from the fact that strong drink was never considered as an ingredient, the whole event was taking on an air of carnival which bade fair to put into the shade the coronation of George VI and the wedding of James to my father's cousin Mary. The latter had been the first wedding in the village and my crony Gillespie and I had been banned from it because it would have been unseemly for five-year-olds to witness their parents abandoning themselves to carousal. But Gillespie and I had sneaked in on the proceedings unnoticed and – not for the last time, though for other reasons – I had spent a convivial evening under a table. But there were no exclusions from the kirk soiree. 'Suffer the little children …' and all the rest of it, provided they were willing to put some effort into the preparations. A couple of members of the Grazings

Committee had tentatively suggested that the lambs could be lifted before the Moderator's day, but they were chided for being so worldly that they could even think of lambs with the man of God about to descend on us. Instead, the Grazings Committee was put to the task of coaxing six crofters to volunteer to donate a farrow sheep each to be slaughtered to feed the multitudes, and when Sandy Cravat had tried to make some facetious remark about loaves and fishes when one of his father's fattest sheep was earmarked for slaughter, Murdo Mor roasted him with a fusillade of biblical quotations that would have done justice to a concordance. The sacrifice of fat sheep seemed highly appropriate and in the best traditions of the Old Testament – except to those who were expected to forego the price that such sheep could command at the autumn sales.

There hadn't been many festive occasions since the village had been founded. Two weddings (of which I remember only James's), the Silver Jubilee in 1935 (still commemorated on countless tea caddies), and the Coronation. These had been celebrated with song and dance, music and flags; but there was a general feeling that the first three of those were not appropriate to an ecclesiastical visitation even if it was taking place on a weekday. But there were still yards of bunting lying around in odd corners, and dyed pillow-cases and table-cloths; even the occasional Union Jack. Were they appropriate or not? That was one of the questions which vexed the village organising committee and not even Murdo Mor knew the answer since the Moderator of the Church of Scotland had never been known to visit Manchester. The widow MacQueen was on the village committee as an ex-officio member by virtue of the fact that she had once been active in the now dormant branch of the WRI, but she had never been known to voice an opinion – having had it explained to her that 'ex-officio' meant 'beholding with charity, and listening in silence'. But when she watched the committee getting into a brangle over the matter of flags she could contain herself no longer. She heaved herself to her feet.

'We will rejoice in thy salvation, and in the name of our God we will set up our banners.'

She sat down, adding as she did so, 'Psalm 20, Verse 5'.

There was a moment of surprised silence. Murdo Mor

glanced left and right as if looking for guidance and then put his fingertips together and looked up at the ceiling which, of course, is where he should have looked in the first place.

'Seconded,' he said. 'Lift ye up a banner upon the high mountain … Isaiah, Chapter 13, Verse 2.'

That decided it; and if Murdo Mor hadn't remembered, in the nick of time, to say, 'Any other business?' everybody would have rushed home to scrabble in odd corners for flags and bamboo fishing rods to hoist them on. However he did remember, and he put the question as he closed the book where he kept his meticulous minutes, fully expecting the usual shuffle of feet and the rush for the door. But instead, the gentlest, quietest man in the Southlands got to his feet – a man who had never been known to utter in public, partly because of his own retiring nature and partly because he was burdened with an impediment of which he was painfully self-conscious.

'Wh-wh-wh-what,' he said, 'about a c-c-c-car for the M-M-M-M-?'

There was no need for him to struggle further. Those who had stood up sat down again, and those who had been silent all evening broke into hubbub. Murdo Mor looked like a man caught with his trousers round his ankles. 'Yes,' he said, 'er – yes …' But he was saved further embarrassment by big George MacLellan, normally not his best friend because MacLellan was a staunch Liberal while Murdo considered the Tory Party more in keeping with his standing as a retired ex-salesman who read the *Glasgow Herald*.

'I'll tell you one thing,' said big Geordie, lumbering to his feet. 'There's no bloody Lewisman going to come the hoity-toity on us by driving the Moderator to Harris; not even if I have to go for him in the Armstrong myself for free.' He sat down amid a ripple of interest, indeed relief. Geordie was the proud possessor of an aged Armstrong Siddley which had once belonged to a Clan Chief who had fallen on evil times. It was far too big for our roads and it took all George's strength to pull it round hairpin bends, but it was an impressive vehicle with hide upholstery (which he pronounced eupholstery) and, occasionally, he hired himself and the car to an unsuspecting tourist or a commercial traveller incautious enough not to check his charges in advance. Usually he used it to ferry livestock between his own and his father's crofts. Nobody had ever known him to offer it to anybody for free.

'And would you promise to give it a polish and a clean inside, George?' asked the Widow MacQueen, encouraged by her earlier first foray into public debate.

The question assumed that Geordie's offer would be accepted, and made it impossible for it to be refused. Geordie not only promised to have the Armstrong polished 'till you couldn't tell it from a bloody Rolls-Royce' but he undertook to wear his Sunday suit and use his Sunday language. Once that was established the whole business of the Moderatorial visit seemed to be complete, and the meeting was on the point of skailing when the Widow MacQueen (who appeared to be smitten by a bug of public oratory) suggested that the meeting be closed with prayer. That is one of the few requests that it is impossible to deny.

On the evening before the day the western sky was red with promise; here and there men went quietly about the business of hauling up flags which just folded back peacefully against their poles; it was so quiet that you could hear a faraway man whistling quietly to himself as he worked, and even the sandpiper sounded sleepy for a change. Over the village hung an aroma of roasting mutton like the sleepy smell of incense over the Plains of Lasithi on the eve of the festival of Agias Zónis. The only note of discord was sounded by the hammer of 'Daft Jimmie' from Drumpound as he laboured at the schoolhouse to fix up two garish notices reading LADDIES and JENTS.

By mid-morning the first of the spectators began to arrive. Few came as strangers because the village had, after all, been created from different parts of the island and grafted on to an indigenous population from which, in turn, relatives had branched out over previous generations. But only the elderly availed themselves of the hospitality of the village homes; most of the visitors came en fête and headed for the school (where Jimmie's notices had been hastily draped with a Lion Rampant and a Union Jack) and there they revelled in tea and coffee and home baking with scant regard for their appetites for the full meal which would follow in the afternoon. The lively frocks of the younger women, mixing with the sedate Sunday suits of the men, reflected exactly the blend of festivity and solemnity which the occasion warranted and got. As the afternoon tiptoed in people moved, automatically, towards the stone-pillared gate leading up to the church on the hillside, and there must have been well over five hundred people assembled there, quietly jostling for the better view, as Big Geordie's Armstrong Siddley appeared, gleaming, over the top of Back of Scarista Hill. He had a feeling for the theatrical moment, had Geordie, and he drove at a carefully measured speed which was halfway between the one he would choose for a wedding and that demanded for a funeral. A silence drifted over the crowd as the big car eased to a halt. Geordie jumped out with a smooth agility of which nobody had ever suspected him. As he opened the rear door nearest the church gates he touched his forehead and stood back waiting for his passenger to get out. The crowd instinctively eased back as a tall, athletic man in a dark coat and a crisp black Anthony Eden hat stepped out and stood surveying the crowd for a moment before addressing George.

'What the bloody hell's going on here?'

The silence froze ten degrees further, except for the aged Agnes MacKenzie from Obbe who spoke no English. She murmured 'Amen'.

Chapter Three

There was no tradition of lynching parties in Harris, there being no trees. But big Geordie would have escaped anyway by divine intervention because, before the crowd had time to draw its corporate breath, there was a suggestion of huzza from somewhere and when we turned to look there was the kenspeckle stately Daimler from Stornoway cruising down the hill, followed by a tail of assorted cars which turned out to contain a whole witness of assorted ministers. This time the assembled company didn't have time to prepare its reaction; as the Daimler drew up the passenger door swung open and a cheery-faced, silver-haired man stepped smartly out, waving a tricorn hat and calling a good humoured Gaelic greeting to the throng. He struck a laughing theatrical pose for a few moments, giving people time to admire his lace jabot and cuffs, frock-coat, breeches, and silver buckled shoes, then he turned round with a sweep of his arm towards the spread of white beach and Atlantic. 'What a lovely place you have here,' he said. 'It's almost as nice as Tiree.' With that, a bodyguard of clerics forcing rusty smiles closed round him and began to urge him through the company towards the church.

No amount of shoe-horn tactics could possibly get everybody into the church although it had been built to accommodate four hundred in the days of its greatness, but somebody managed to open windows that hadn't opened for generations and soon the spine-tingling sound of precented

Gaelic psalm welled out from the ancient walls and was lifted by the crowd outside to the older hills. In moments of memory, when the noises of the village drift back to me across the years – the corncrake, the bleat of lambs, the clack of looms, soughing winds and grumbling sea – there peeps through, just once in a sacred while, an echo of 'Ye gates lift up your heads on high ...' as it rose to the skies that day.

When the Moderator climbed to the pulpit he took as his text, 'But when ye hear of wars and commotions, be not terrified.' And he preached a sermon of peace and comfort on the subject that men were trying to push to the back of their minds at that time. He knew what he was talking about because he had been through the same war as the men who had founded our village, and, like them, he hoped not to see another.

The service was short – or, at least, felt short in comparison with the ones to which we had become accustomed from a series of lay preachers during the period of our own kirk's fallowness – and when it was over, he broke away from his entourage and wandered among the people, cracking jokes in his own native Gaelic, which had a tinge of foreignness to us. Old ladies who had moulded their faces in preparation for an eminence of divinity found their legs being pulled about this and that; he attempted to swop hats with the Widow MacQueen, but hers was anchored to her head with a pin that would have held a sail in a storm; he asked a blushing teenager if she was married and offered to send her a list of eligible bachelors from Tiree; and in his more serious moments he revealed a remarkable knowledge of the affairs of the parish and hoped that we would find a minister of our own soon. At last one of his companions tugged his sleeve anxiously and suggested that they were falling behind schedule and should be getting on their way. 'What!' he said. 'And not sample that cooking I smelt as we passed the school?' And that, in itself, was enough to endear him to the women who had devoted time and care to preparing the spread.

Down in the school the two-seater desks had been draped in white cloths and were laden with enough food to feed a multitude without the invocation of miracle. The Moderator wandered among them, picking a mutton sandwich from one,

41

a buttered oatcake here and a pancake there, and demanding constant re-fills of tea. The only man who did more justice to the bill of fare was a tall, athletic man, incongruously dressed for the sunshine in a dark coat and a black Anthony Eden hat, who had uttered only one sentence since he had arrived in the village, but it was destined to be remembered more vividly than the Moderator's text from St Luke.

'Who the hell's that?' somebody at last managed to whisper to big Geordie MacLellan, who had gone through the proceedings with a sullen expression that had hung like a thunder-cloud on a sunny day.

'I don't know who the bugger is,' gritted Geordie. 'He was standing outside St Columba Church in Stornoway with a suitcase, and when I stopped he asked me if I was the driver from Scarista. I couldn't get a word out of him the whole way down except grumbles about how long the journey was taking, and the poor bloody Armstrong doing forty –' He twitched on a smile that didn't reach his eyes as the Moderator drifted over and asked him what he did for a living.

'Who's the bloody half-wit with the Armstrong Siddley?' asked the man in the Anthony Eden hat when he felt that the Moderator was out of earshot.

The Boer War veteran pretended that he didn't know.

'I was standing on the pavement outside the County Hotel when he pulled up and when I asked him if he was the driver from Scaliscro he told me he was. I was due at an important meeting at Scaliscro Lodge at midday, but that fellow's getting me back there if it's midnight when we arrive. God knows what trouble he's caused!'

'Ach well, so long as you enjoyed yourself. I saw them giving you a seat at the front of the church seeing you were a stranger –'

'I happen to be a Roman Catholic. And I don't speak Gaelic!'

'And what's a man without Gaelic doing in these parts?' The Boer War veteran was a chatty, friendly man.

'I'm from the War Department.'

'Ach well,' said the old man tamping his pipe to hide the twinkle in his eye. 'Just once in a while it can be a good thing not to understand Gaelic.'

42

The man from the War Department looked puzzled, but decided to move towards the sandwiches while the Boer War veteran continued smiling to himself, remembering that the County Hotel and St Columba Church were, indeed, on the same street in Stornoway and that, in Geordie MacLellan's vocabulary 'outside' was an elastic sort of a word.

At long last the Moderator yielded to the supplications of his acolytes and allowed himself to be propelled gently towards the waiting Daimler which eased him off in the direction of his next appointment, having won for himself the love of a whole community and leaving behind him an aura of blessing and goodwill. As soon as his car moved off the company erupted into a chatter of relief and self-congratulation and the comparing of notes. Nobody paid any attention to the children descending on the remains of the feast; and only the Boer War veteran had noticed the agility with which the man in the Anthony Eden hat had flung himself into the back of the Armstrong Siddley as big Geordie tried to make his escape in the wake of the Moderator's convoy. In their twos and threes the visitors from other villages began to say their farewells; hired buses revved their engines and belched smoke, impatiently summoning their respective detachments of Women's Rural Institutes, Fishermen's Associations, and Congregational Boards to climb aboard. Grandparents and uncles and aunts would linger on for a day or two, taking advantage of the rare excuse for a holiday in the Southlands; but, by and large, the excitement which had taken weeks to bring its climax was ebbing pleasurably around us as we stood.

It was Farquhar the roadman who finally brought reality thudding back. 'Hey, children!' he shouted. 'Don't scoff every last morsel just because it's there; leave some over for the fank tomorrow. The least you can do is save your poor mothers some work after all they've been through already, and into the bargain give us a better picnic than usual at the fank.' There was a murmur of approval from adults of both sexes and the men loosened their ties and flung off their jackets as they began to give a hand restoring the schoolroom to normal as the women folded away table-cloths and napery for washing or else packed the remaining food into parcels for the next day.

'Do you think the weather's going to hold then?' somebody asked Farquhar, who had the reputation of being good at reading the skies.

'No doubt about it,' he replied. 'The Moderator's going to be in the islands for two days yet, and he's the kind for whom good weather lasts!'

It was a great tribute for a man who had a reputation for being 'worldly' and grudging a sunny Sabbath as a wasted working day.

When the last remains of the food had been rescued from them, the youngsters scattered away to play. For my part I was left awaiting a request to help here or there, but for the most part just listening, or answering the occasional question that someone might occasionally fling my way. More and more the awkward loneliness of adolescence was beginning to haunt me; I was very tall for my age and what was referred to despairingly by teacher and parents alike as my 'slouch' was, I suspect in retrospect, a self-conscious effort to conceal the fact that I was a head taller than my contemporaries; each winter my boot size had jumped by two so that, by now, I was wearing a full size larger than my father. For lack of anything better to do I would still, occasionally, seek to join in the pastimes of my younger brothers and their contemporaries but I couldn't help but be contemptuous of their attempts at whatever imaginary edifices or citadels they were trying to create, nor could I avoid using crude logic to scorn their fantasies; the result was that they evolved ways of making it clear that they didn't want my company and I would be left to wander off on my own like a gawky pup rejected by frolicking kittens – hurt more by the snub than the scratches.

Because I had failed to win the bursary to High School at my first attempt my pride was hurt anyway, but what made things worse was that my immediate contemporaries, who had either left school or had moved on to High School, had suddenly become denizens of another world – a world of adulthood in which they were either labourers in vineyards in which they earned their keep, or, what was even more difficult to accept, knowledgeable snobs who came back to the village on holiday, wearing good shoes and using English swear-words even, occasionally, in front of their parents; and though their smoking was still secret they held their cigarettes elegantly between the tips of their first and second fingers and blew the smoke out slowly through their noses. I marvelled at how quickly higher education lifted people into a different social class and I could only steel myself to wait for the day when I could join it.

At home things were little better. My father – who had been parent and friend and subtle mentor – had been delighted when I had won the scholarship, but, almost overnight, the relationship between us had changed; he became impatient with my attempts at adult conversation, sceptical of my arguments, and angry at my contradictions. Was I too much of a gentleman to wind bobbins for his loom? Would I deign to weave a couple of yards of tweed while he did some croftwork, and if I did would it be too much to expect that if I got a false 'cross-thread' I would spare time to correct it rather than ruin his reputation as a weaver? Would it ruin my golf swing if I exercised my back to bring home a sack of peat from the hillside? Sometimes I felt the blood rush to my face and the tears swelling my eyelids as I bit them back and wished that he would just ask me to do things wheedlingly or sly-humouredly as he used to do: at other times I was angry with myself that I couldn't keep an edge of insolence out of the tone in which I spoke to him. My mother's attitude had altered less, except that, occasionally, she got tired of getting caught in the cross-fire and she would order me to get out from under her feet when she found me, after yet another brush with my father, crouched in a corner with a book.

Books were becoming an essential leaven of my being instead of just the indulgence of pleasure to which my father himself had led me; but because we had never got out of the small hut which had been supposed to be temporary when it had been built ten years before, and because the family had increased in number and in bulk, privacy was hard to find. On fine days I could occasionally escape down to the rocky shore of the Blue Skerries with the volume of the moment tucked under my ganzie, and I would lose track of time and place till the pangs of hunger or the prickles of conscience would urge me home. Books were an escape from everything, even though they were few and far between; Edgar Wallace, Algernon

45

Blackwood, Annie S Swan, O Douglas, Leslie Charteris all plucked at different chords of the imagination as they became available in the wooden crates delivered to the school by the County Lending Library; those moulded and catered for the admissible curiosities: the ever gnawing pangs of sexuality which could find no physical outlet in the village, nor prurient gratification in the carefully vetted volumes of the library, had to be satisfied by the occasional dog-eared volume brought home by one of my seaman cousins – literary titillates like *No Orchids for Miss Blandish* or *The Awful Confessions of Maria Monk*.

The abrasion of the special relationship with my father saddened me although I didn't understand it as sadness then; the only sadness now is that it never got a chance to heal because of time and inexorable circumstances – except for a brief spell, and through unusual circumstances, four years later. I learnt – as every man learns in time – that part of the tension was the inevitable father and son spasm of puberty; it took me longer to understand that there was an Oedipus strand in reverse, and that it was bitter for him to see his own son escaping from what he was beginning to accept as his own imprisonment. God knows what reactions to those years of war had deluded him into thinking that a new croft in a new land would ever provide the fulfilment for which he craved; whatever they were they were as illusory as the geographical change for the alcoholic. He was, heart and mind, a man of books and letters, and it was only natural that his joy would be tempered with envy, and his own frustration more sharply focussed, by seeing the first of his family getting the chance to embark on the sort of life for which he himself craved, and in which he would have thrived.

Conversely, my relationships in the village strengthened in those difficult weeks during which my enforced idleness and my suspension between two worlds were both factors exacerbating the difficulties between my father and myself. Other parents are always more able to sympathise with the problems of other people's children than they are with those of their own, and where I was finding it increasingly difficult to communicate with my father I was finding it easier to talk to people like the Boer War veteran, who had a smile for every boy. There was the man who had decided to emigrate to Patagonia in his own boyhood, but had seized on the offer of a government-sponsored free passage to return home to volunteer for the navy in 1914; when other people were preaching the gospel of 'get up and get out and get on' he alone was adamant that there was a future for young people in our own island. 'After all,' he used to say. 'I've been and I've seen, and the grass was no greener.' The man with the hole in his cheek was a listener of infinite patience and the mark of the bullet always made me feel that the brush with death had given a new dimension to his wisdom: his wife was one of the early innocent loves of my life. She could keep up a sparkling conversation without making one feel callow, and she always had all the time in the world although she never sat down in a house where everything always shone. Whenever I pass the home where she lived, as I do all too rarely now, I can still imagine the taste of the Atholl Brose (sans alcohol) that she conjured from fine oatmeal and the freshest of fresh cream that she distilled from unfermented milk with the new-fangled separator in which she had invested to the astonishment of older women who had spent their days setting basins and waiting for the cream to rise. Alas I can only imagine the taste because she died long, long ago, and far too young. There were others too – men and women I had known from the day that the new village had begun on the site of the old one. Most of all, there was, of course, Old Hector whose life consisted entirely of spare time.

On the day of the Moderator's visit I had made several efforts to catch Old Hector on his own so that I could find out whether the postman had brought a reply to our advertisement. But he seemed to be in popular demand and every time I got within earshot of him somebody else intervened and engaged him in conversation. I tried catching his eye and raising my eyebrows in question, but all I got back was an exasperating blank stare. I could hardly wait for milking time to come, and when I did finally prepare to set off my father remarked, 'You're in a devil of a hurry to milk Hector's cow tonight; I wish I could see you jumping to it when I ask you to do something around the croft.' I couldn't think of a reply and left the house, conscious once again, that by not responding I had created, quite unintentionally, a suggestion of deliberate insolence. It was always the way things seemed to work out. But, for sure, I couldn't tell him why I was so keen to see Old Hector.

He was sitting crouched over his fire in the middle of the floor when I arrived; he was looking very morose, and my first reaction was that he had received a rejection.

'Are you going off your head? How the devil could I get a refusal when nobody knows what I did? I'm the only proposer in history who can only get an acceptance, and that's what's worrying me. I didn't get anything. That bloody Calum the Post could conjure up a holiday out of a summer shower! As soon as he heard of the Moderator's visit he was going round the place declaring a public holiday for himself, and saying it wouldn't be right for a public servant to be trundling the roads in a red van during a religious festival. Religious festival my backside! He doesn't even belong to the Church of Scotland ...' He spat towards the fire and missed – sure proof that he was out of kilter. I hadn't realised that there hadn't been a mail delivery that day, but it didn't surprise me; Calum didn't require much excuse to cancel his northward delivery trip and jam his delivery and collection trips into the following day. He was a man of measured tread in a community upon which the Royal Mail had not impressed urgency. But the old man's next question did catch me unawares.

'What made you tell your mother?'

'Me! I didn't tell my mother or anybody else.' I bridled at the very thought that he could suspect me. 'What on earth makes you think such a rotten thought?'

'I heard her discussing it with Hetty MacInnes – that's what. Down in the schoolhouse when they were waiting for the Moderator to arrive for his tea. I wasn't able to get into the church so I thought I might as well make something of the day, and I slipped down to the school to make sure that I got a bite to eat at least. And the two of them were in spate and laughing their heads off; they shut up as soon as they saw me.'

'What were they saying?'

'Your mother was going on about there being no fool like an old fool; and Hetty was saying "There's something romantic about it too; him up there all alone in his wee house waiting for

48

a letter from the woman of his dreams –" and she stopped and went as red as a beetroot when she saw me ...'

I burst out laughing before he could finish his sentence. I had been short of reading material and I'd been following the serial in the *People's Friend*, the weekly women's magazine which my mother and Hetty shared. I recognised the description of the ageing Dr Dalhousie waiting to hear from the childhood sweetheart with whom he had managed to make contact after forty years, to find that she was still unmarried.

'You may be right in thinking of yourself as an old fool,' I said. 'But you've got a great conceit to be thinking you're the only one. My mother and Hetty were talking about a story from a women's magazine!'

He looked relieved, but I felt a qualm of conscience yet again as it was brought home to me how much the whole thing was preying on Old Hector's mind. He was obviously going through his every day fearful of the result of what I always regarded as 'our advertisement' and even more fearful that any of the villagers would guess at the identity of 427. What I did appreciate (and he didn't) was that every post office in the Hebrides was not necessarily thronged with eager females jostling to catch the first postal collection with an acceptance of a vague and rather dubious proposal of marriage from some unknown person with a number instead of a name. But, on the other hand, I hadn't foreseen some of the problems that had suggested themselves to Hector during his sleepless hours.

'What happens if the most promising reply comes from a Roman Catholic?'

'You ignore it. You tear up the letter.'

'Very smart. But do you really think she's going to say right away that she's a Catholic; after all, you didn't say we wanted a Protestant woman, did you?'

I was thoroughly tired of the way the burden of responsibility was thrust on me whenever he got jittery.

'I didn't say I wanted anybody; I'm not a *retired seaman*. If the best reply comes from a Roman Catholic you'll just have to convert – that's that!'

'Damnation, you really are out of your senses. There's been only one Roman Catholic in Harris ever, and I'm not going to be the third. In any case I'd have to convert *to* the Church of

Scotland before I could convert out of it. I've never been anything special – just a fellow who goes to church on a Sunday if the day's good –'

I wasn't quick enough to point out to him that becoming a Catholic would absolve him from even casual attendance since there was no Catholic Church in the island. In any case, I had just remembered another problem, and I cut in before he could expand on his church attitudes.

'Hey, just wait. There's something else. Do you realise that the *Gazette* doesn't sell only in the Outer Hebrides; it goes to Glasgow and London and Canada? And my auntie sends her copy to a cousin in West Africa when she's read it herself.'

He looked at me to see if I was joking, and decided that I wasn't.'

'So now you're trying to tell me she could be Catholic and black!'

'No, I'm not saying that. Although it could be true it's not likely. What I'm trying to say is that the mail takes a long time crossing the Atlantic and you might have to wait a month or more for a letter from, say, Canada –'

His eyes were glittering and he had allowed his pipe to go out. I knew he was getting angry, but I couldn't find a way out of a conversation which he himself had started. But I did, quite sincerely, have a vision (improbable though it might be) of Hector finding himself a nice, decent, wife with a streak of jealousy in her who would have to add to the other hazards of her early marriage a steady trickle of letters from the four corners of the world, from panting females of varying creeds and contours offering to marry her husband and bring a dowry of diamonds. I had seen enough old copies of the *News of the World* to know that ever-increasing hazards beset passionate marriages made in Heaven far less postal ones made in Harris.

He stabbed in my direction with his cutty pipe.

'Look here, my boy. Just get this into your head. If any woman is damn fool enough to answer that advertisement, I will size her up from her letter and if I don't like the sound of her the letter goes into the fire there, and I know enough to know that nobody could sue a number for breach of promise even if a promise had been made.' That got that off his chest and he began to re-light his pipe with his modest self-assurance restored. 'And I'll tell you another thing – you yourself have put my mind at ease although that's not what you meant to do; you said that if I got a letter from a Catholic I could tear it up. Well, I can tear up every damn letter that comes if I feel like it. I don't know why I let myself get into these fits of depression – it's from being alone too much. Go and milk the cow!'

I had never heard him being so decisive in his life. I got up without saying a word, picked up the pail, and went out to find Primrose. It was a mark of his new-found self-confidence that he didn't bother to waddle out after me. As I got down to the business of milking I thought to myself that if Old Hector did, by some strange chance, find himself a wife, she'd have to wait a week or two before she found the real Hector. I found myself hoping that the miracle would happen and that a nice woman would come along. Somewhere, there must be one who would be prepared to put up with his shortcomings from the goodness of her heart and *for* the goodness of his. I realised that my affection for him was deeper than pity, and kinder than pity by far.

When I got back into the house he had the little black teapot nestling on a bed of peat embers, and he began to pour as I set the milk. I searched out a reasonably long cigarette dout from behind the plate in his dresser where I kept a secreted supply. He held out the spill with which he had kindled his own pipe.

'Do you know,' he said, 'I was sitting here thinking while you were out at the milking. You were joking about me and a Catholic earlier on, and the thought came to me that maybe the Catholics have something after all. They go in for all that pomp and ceremonial and fancy stuff that the Presbyterians miscall them for, but did you notice how people liked the Moderator today – in all his fancy lace and buckled shoes. I think people secretly fancy a wee bit of colour in their lives, and we're too black and white altogether. Just you look at the Bible which I read more than you think when I'm alone here – it hasn't got a single bad word to say against beauty. It talks about the beauty of the lilies of the field, and the beauty of holiness, and the temple which is called Beautiful. And wasn't it three things of beauty that the wise men brought to the infant Christ?' He stopped and stared into the fire for a long time, and let the pipe in his hand go out. 'And we're blessed with a beautiful village here, you know. We forget it sometimes; it's only when I remember my boyhood that I remember the village as being beautiful – for most of the time I take it for granted; but I remembered the beauty of it that time when I thought I was dying in Singapore – by Jove I remembered it then ...

'You see, boy, I remember this place long before there was any thought of you people coming and settling in it, and it wasn't just beauty we had but happiness too although we were poor and had no land of our own. And one reason was that the kind of minister we had here was always a man of the soil – a man who worked his glebe there, and tended his sheep during the week just like any farmer. He knew what he was talking about. He was never a narrow-minded man ... And then, when you people came, your men were men who had seen danger and war and they wouldn't have put up with bloody-minded holiness. I think that's why there's a problem finding a minister now; the right kind don't come by the dozen. In the end it won't be us who'll find a minister; the right man will find us ...'

He struggled to his feet.

'And that's the gospel according to Old Hector. And that's the end of it ... it's time you were off home, and be back here for Calum the Post coming in the morning!' He patted my shoulder and ushered me out.

My way back home was down past the empty manse and the empty church, and I realised that I had got used to the idea that we didn't have a minister. I'd got used to the village being without one. I didn't even know if they were still looking for one.

As I reached the road the Armstrong Siddley came towards me and passed; the driver never looked my way and I only caught a glimpse of his white face staring straight ahead, but I knew that the look on big Geordie MacLellan's face was the look of a man who had done two hires to Stornoway for free.

I was still smiling to myself when I got into the house.

'Hello lad,' said my father. 'You're looking in a good mood and it's just as well – because we're a man short for the sheep-gathering tomorrow and you're going to have to do the south shoulder with me.'

I stared at him.

'No need to sulk now. A day on the hill will do your lungs a

52

power of good – and your mind too, before you set off to a gentleman's life in High School.'

That was typical of his misunderstanding of my every reaction nowadays. I wasn't sulking. I liked the hill. But I knew that if I went to the hill my mother would have to milk Hector's cow, and I wondered what on earth she would think when Calum the Post arrived with a sack of mail for a man who hadn't been known to receive a letter in years.

Chapter Four

The dawn is always cold underfoot although people with boots don't realise it. It was the rasping of my soles together to get the circulation going that brought my father out of his morning reverie.

'Shouldn't you be putting a pair of boots on for the hill? The heather's beginning to harden and you'll be hobbling like a duck on stubble before the day's half through.'

'I'll be O.K. – I'll be all right.' I corrected myself hastily; O.K. was beginning to creep into Gaelic usage and my father abominated the increasing use of 'Ganglish' which was already beginning to erode our language of every day, and dismissed the younger generation who were succumbing to it as 'illiterates in two languages'.

We were sitting together over our bowls of oatmeal brose and skimmed milk with the kettle beginning to hiss towards a new boil for tea. Although the days of hardship were relatively in the past our diet was still the diet of poverty which has become the diet of many fortunes in modern times. Weekday breakfasts were still oatmeal brose, or porridge, with skimmed milk (the cream being saved up for butter-making) with a boiled egg and oatcakes to follow. The main meal of the day was invariably salt herring and potatoes during the winter, with a switch to fresh fish during the summer depending on the regularity of the 'fish landry' as Montgomery's van had now come to be known. Normally Sunday was the only meat day although, perceptibly, Fray Bentos was not only creeping onto the menu but also into the vocabulary of our every day as the synonym for tinned meat regardless of its constituents or manufacturer. It is interesting but sad to look back over the years and realise that one was present when a language began to go into its death throes. Gaelic had survived the deliberate Government policy which had tried to extinguish it over a century and a half but, in the thirties, the acceleration of scientific progress with its new vernacular, the opening up of the Highlands to tourists, the invasion of newspapers and attractive magazines in English, the importation of 'English' mini-bureaucrats to positions of key importance ... all these things were beginning to undermine people's confidence in their own native language and relegate it in their subconscious to a workaday status, like a worn-out pullover useful for 'around the house' while English was the Sunday suit for high-days and holidays. When packaged foods began to creep in as money became more plentiful they wrought their own particular destructions – why, for example, bother to adapt a Gaelic word when 'loff' was an easy-on-the-tongue corruption for the mainland bread that was arriving in ever-increasing quantities in increasingly attractive and hygienic waxed wrapping and rendering the baking board and the griddle obsolete. The process was just beginning to begin.

'You and your O.K.,' my father said. 'You'll be as bad as the Reverend George before you know where you are!' The 'Reverend George' was one of the lay preachers who came to us on circuit during the period of vacancy in our church; unlike many worthy men who shared the round with him, he had spent a few months at a college before systematically failing a series of exams, but not before acquiring a rare conceit of himself to which he gave expression by interlarding his conversations and sermons with reams of English. 'You get it into your head that your own language is a great and beautiful language,' father went on. 'Some people claim that it was the language spoken in the Garden of Eden but I suspect that that's as doubtful as some of the Reverend George's theology. And English is a language of great power too – and beauty, as you've heard in Lord MacAulay's poetry. But when you mix the two together it's like crossing a sheepdog and a greyhound – you get a mongrel that's good for neither one thing nor another.'

My spirits rose. My father was back to his old form, and in the kind of mood which, over the years, had drawn us most closely together. The day on the hill promised to be good.

As we set off together a wreath of mist was wrapped round the shoulders of Bleaval like a silken scarf. Below, the mountain was purplish brown where the bloom on the heather was already beginning to give way to the autumn. The top, which was chilly on the hottest summer day, was etched grey and back-lit by the sun, which had already risen but hadn't yet cleared the top of the mountain, and I knew that by the time we reached the highest point of the ridge we'd be glad of the bottles of whey my father was carrying in his make-shift knapsack. Neither of us spoke except that, once in a while, he'd mutter to Fraoch to keep to heel; the dog had been this way before and he was restless and twitching to get on with his job of rounding up the sheep. He was a loveable, loyal animal and would follow any of the family through fire, but my father was a notoriously bad trainer and poor Fraoch had none of those finely honed techniques that will take a sheepdog snaking over a mile of moorland, tuned in to whistles too silent for the human ear, to separate one particular sheep from a flock. We would walk three times the distance that some of the crofters would do; we would have to get behind the sheep in order to drive them in while some of the more skilled neighbours would get their dogs to bring the sheep to them. For that reason, I suspected, we were given the easiest beat, and it was face-saving good fortune that it happened to be the one most geographically convenient to our croft. Now and again, in the distance, I could hear an occasional cough or a discreet whistle: I knew that along the foot of the mountain eight men were climbing, careful not to disturb the sheep till they were able to cordon them off at the mountain top in order to sweep them back down before them towards the fank at the Brown Shore.

When our village had been founded, the Board of Agriculture had ordained a souming of fifty sheep per crofter; that being calculated to be the number – a total of five hundred and fifty including the landlord's hundred and the minister's fifty – that the in-bye and the moorland grazing could sustain.

But recent landlords hadn't been interested in sheep and we'd had no minister for a while so the more adventurous crofters had quietly allowed their sheepstock to expand; even the less adventurous couldn't be expected to be highly numerate when it suited themselves not to be and the souming was now given only token observance. That day we would expect to bring some eight hundred sheep off the hill, including the season's lambs. In the townsman's legend sheep are stupid animals, but that is far from being the case, as any shepherd knows who has seen the understanding look in a sheep's eye as he tries to help her with a difficult lambing. And they have a highly developed sense of territory. Although we were bounded on three sides by other townships, there were no boundary fences; yet it was rarely that one of our sheep strayed off our mountain or one of our neighbours' animals wandered over to us. And when one did, it was, often as not, a sheep that had been sold from one township to another – or even its descendant – that was returning home. The sheep that we passed, nestled in the heather, on our way up the hill, were newly wakened and chewing their morning cud; they gazed at us incuriously without stirring, as much as to say, 'We know what you're up to; we'll see you on your way back!' Only the lambs, who were new to the game, showed flinches of panic and rushed to their dams.

The mist seemed to be retreating in front of us as we climbed, and when we finally reached the top edge of Bleaval's shoulder the day was crystal clear. Even while the sun was hot on the top of one's head one could feel the pinch of the mountain air on one's face. We had taken a good hour to reach our point of return, but it would take some of the men who were going to the summit another half-hour and they would take half an hour's rest then; so we had a good hour to wait. We sat down and my father unscrewed the top out of one of the bottles of whey. The scene was one that was familiar to me, and when I see it now, occasionally, from the cramped seat of an aeroplane, it comes as an illogical shock that it hasn't changed, and I fancy that if I could conjure up a whiff of that sharp mountain air time would roll back with the memory. But alas ...

Behind us the back of Bleaval sloped down to the

fragmented, craggy coast and coves of the Eastlands and the shores of the Minch. Thither, a hundred years ago, our forebears from our village and its neighbours had been evicted to make way for the sheepfarms. There, among the selfish rocks, they had built up, laboriously over the years, with seaweed and scraped soil, the isolated little patches of fertility in which they had grown their potatoes and their tussocks of corn. Here and there they had drained small marshes and rescued slivers of arable land. With aching backs they had created oases among the Lewisian gneiss – enough to feed themselves along with the fish they could haul from the Minch. In the same way as we had returned ourselves to the west from the Northlands, so the descendants of those people had returned too, and created new villages along the coast from our own. But that had only been a thinning of the east coast population; down there in the morning light the patches among the rocks were still green with new corn, and smoke was rising from the modern new homes that had sprung up. But even then we knew that the Eastlands were living on loaned time, and without sufficient land and without any hopes of industry the population would age and shrink as life came to depend more and more on 'folding money'. The Minch was rich in fish still but, already, the rumbling and grumblings were beginning about invading trawlers scraping it clean.

Beyond the Minch lay the deceptive mountains of Skye – pale grey and listless in the morning light like old ladies resting on their elbows, but it needed only a gust of north wind ruffling down the Minch, or a scudding cloud across the sun to change them into hard-edged, lowering menace. I've seen it happening to them from that aeroplane seat, and that way too – even in their sudden ability to change – there is a continuity. And, behind the Coolins, the mountains of Ross and Sutherland, culminating in the grandeur of Cuil Beg, Cuil Mor, Arkle and Canisp … I never could get the order right, and there seems to be little need to now!

In front, one could have been looking out on another world. It was a surprise to be reminded how far we had climbed; our own huge beach that filled the entire view from the window of home was only one bay among several now, and the breakers on it that I knew to be high and foaming looked like a gentle white frill on a web of blue that stretched out to infinity, broken only here and there by specks of islands that the distance had stripped of character. To the right, peeping out from behind the Point of Huisinis but many miles away, the Flannan Isles; in the centre, Gaisgeir; and to the far left and furthest still away, St Kilda – empty by then, but once a valued piece of Clan MacLeod territory yielding rents that were well worth the collecting.

It was the movement that broke my day-dream as my father put the stopper back into the whey bottle, drew the back of his hand across his lips, and felt for his pipe. His eyes were narrowed as he gazed out across the miles to where the sea and sky met in such a compatibility of colour that there was no defined horizon. There was a crinkle of smile at the corner of his mouth, and I knew from experience that he was going to embark on one of his long discourses – yarn, fable, or theory, since there was no cause for exhortation or upbraiding.

'It's strange –' he said, and paused. 'Strange to think that somewhere away out there there's a whole country swallowed up with all its people by the sea.'

'What do you mean?'

He pretended to look surprised. 'What do you mean by "what do you mean?" You're not going to tell me you don't know about it?'

'No. I don't.'

'You've never heard of Neil-who-got-lost?'

'Never.'

'Well, well, well … It was my own grandfather who told me the story – the old man they called the Cleric – and I wouldn't be surprised if it was right on this spot that he told me. You see, I used to come here from the Northlands to visit my old grandfather on my mother's side in the same way as you've been going back to the Northlands to visit your Big Grandfather for the last few summers. And I used to climb Bleaval with him just as we've done today – not to gather sheep or anything like that, but just because the old man liked to come up to the top of the mountain and, as he got older, he used to say that I was good at finding the easiest ways to the top …

'According to him Neil-who-got-lost was one of the few

59

men who ever worked a boat out from these shores; as you know it's almost impossible to work a boat out from an exposed sandy beach like ours although I believe natives in the South Sea Islands manage to cope with bigger breakers than we ever see. Anyway, although Neil-who-got-lost (nobody knew any other name for him even in the Cleric's day) was a great dreamer and a great seaman at the same time and it's not often those two characteristics go together. He got himself a little boat – a coracle made with hides, which shows you how long ago it was – and he worked her out from the Red Geo where we fish for cuddies and saithe nowadays. God knows there's not much shelter there, but it's better than the open beach and the coracle was so light that he could climb up the rocks with it on his back like a snail with its shell.

'In those days men didn't have crofts to tie them down, and every day that was fine for fishing at all Neil-who-got-lost (that wasn't the name they knew him by then, of course) would launch his coracle and get out behind the breakers and sit fishing there in the middle of the bay, just catching enough shelter from Toe Head to make his long sit comfortable. Goodness only knows what he thought about, as he sat there for hour after hour with a line over the side, hauling in a cod now and again, or a lythe or a ling, because fish were plentiful in those days and with the coast being so bad hereabouts there was nobody to disturb them. Perhaps he made songs to pass the time for himself when the fish weren't biting – the old Cleric didn't know, because, of course, if he made songs they got lost with him. Sometimes on a particularly quiet day he would sit out in his coracle till the dusk came down and then he would row quietly back to the Red Geo. As you know yourself the sea is never quieter than when the tide is full on a still, calm evening.

'There came an evening, however, when Neil lost track of time and place all together, and when he came to himself he realised that a whiff of a breeze from the land had crept up on him unawares and that he was drifting away out past Toe Head. Not that that worried him at first; he was a good oarsman and he had been out that far often enough before. He thought that all he had to do was put the oars on her and pull a little harder than usual and keep pulling – the way any wise man does when things aren't going his way. But it wasn't just as easy for Neil as he thought. The sky had been darkening without his noticing it, and a stiff cold breeze was strengthening from the east and giving courage to the tide as they say, and, row as he might, Neil was making no headway and at last he realised that he'd be wise to save what strength he had left till he found a more hopeful purpose for it. He shipped his oars and lay down on the bottom of the boat so as to give the breeze less to get hold of.

'Now there isn't a sound in the world as sleep-making as the slip-slapping of the sea on the side of a boat if you're not the kind of person who worries about it; and Neil certainly wasn't that. Without knowing he was doing it he fell asleep, and when he woke up he thought he had just dozed off for a few moments because when you don't know whether the sun's in the east or in the west it's very difficult to tell the dusk from the dawn. But when the day began to get brighter instead of darker the man in the boat realised that he had slept the night through, and he wouldn't have been mortal if he hadn't been worried when he couldn't see a glimpse of land in front of him or behind him or on either side. There are, in life, times when there is nothing you can do to help yourself. People will tell you otherwise, but it's true – times in fact, when by trying to do something you are only making your state of affairs worse. That's where men who have a belief are lucky. They just sit back and let God take over, and, whatever happens – be it to their own good or their bad – they say that it was God's will.

'I don't know what Neil did, but, for sure, he drifted for three days and he could hardly believe his eyes when he woke up one morning and found himself almost ashore on a beautiful white strand on the greenest island he had ever seen. For a moment or two, when he saw the white beach, he thought he was back home again; but there was something about the green-ness of the land which convinced him that this was a place he had never seen in his life before. But what could he do? He wasn't going to push off and start rowing, was he? That would have been both the height and the depth of madness at the same time. No. He did what any man would do; he stepped ashore and pulled the coracle up behind him – so high up that no tide would reach it no matter how high

61

might be the tides that they had in a place like that.

'He was just on the point of wandering off to see what he could see when a light finger of fear touched him lest this might be the kind of place where mortals didn't thrive, and with the fear came memory of the knife in his pocket – a knife on which a wise old woman had once put a charm to protect him from evil, and just to be on the safe side he took the knife and buried it in the sand two paces to the left of the stone to which he had tied the coracle, and three paces ahead. And he set off on his search for whatever might be there that he couldn't see. He hadn't gone far when he met people who greeted him with smiles and with kindness, and gave him food to eat and drink to drink; but when he asked them where he was they just looked at him with faraway looks in their eyes and talked round his question without ever coming to the answer. And that's how it was for days. The farther he wandered the more beautiful the land became, and round each corner there was sunshine and never a trace of shadow.

'Well, I needn't tell you what happened. One of those days he met a woman who was as young as the rest but even more beautiful, and when she smiled at him it was as if he had known her all his life and wanted to get to know her more. And in due course they got married – not by a minister or a priest because there was no such person that he could see, but a man who seemed to be a little older than the rest; not in the way he looked or in the way he walked but, somehow, in the way he seemed to think. And the years went by – or the days, rather, because you can't count years when there are no winters. He was happy but not fully happy, and he kept wondering to himself why not; then one night a truth came to him out of the back of his mortal memory and he remembered that his happinesses from the past had been because he had always had sadnesses against which to measure them. And the more he thought about it, the more disjaskit his thinking became and he got to the stage when he couldn't sleep a full night nor keep awake a full day. Then, suddenly – and it was the first sudden thing that had happened to him in that place – he began to long for home, and for simple things like a glimpse of Bleaval on which we're sitting here, and a shower of rain, a flake of crotal on a rock, the sound of a storm, and the things that you and I take for granted and sometimes don't even like. The longing grew in him like a tubercle in the soul and, at last, he said to the woman of his life, *Come with me, back to my country and my people; I want to show them the beautiful bride that I've found for myself, and I want to show them to you.*

'She looked at him with her eyes full of the first clouding that he had ever seen there, and he felt a pain in his heart for having troubled her. *You've got the madness of mortals*, she said. *I'll go to the ends of our world here with you but not a step beyond, for I will never be part of that craziness that makes your kind want to go searching out sorrow the instant they've found content. And even if I wanted to go with you are you foolish enough to think that they'd let us?*

'In the very business of thinking human thoughts again, human cunning came back to him, and for the first time in their life together he set out to deceive her. *All right*, he said. *I accept the wisdom of what you're saying, and it was madness that made me talk the way I did. But at least come down to my boat with me and let's go for a plowter round the bay; I've got a great yearning to feel oars in my hands again.*

'She looked at him with love back in her eyes again. *If that'll make you happy it's not much to ask and even less for me to give. Let's do that thing for your happiness, but for your greater happiness, put out of your mind any hope or thought of hope that you'll ever get beyond the outer reef at the mouth of the bay. Perhaps the very tiredness of the oars in your hands will be the thing that'll teach you forevermore to be content with the good fortune you've got.*

'They went down together, and he was pleased beyond telling to see that his boat was just as he had left it, without any trace of rot or decay or sign of the length of time she had been there. Even the oars were just as he had placed them. He went to the stone to which he had tied the mooring rope, and he took two paces to the left of the stone and then turned and took three paces straight ahead of him, and when his companion wasn't looking he bent down and scooped the charmed knife out of the sand where he had hidden it and put it in his pocket. *Take a hold of one gunwale*, he said. *And together we'll carry her to the water.* She laughed and did as he told her. *It'll be the first and the last time of my life*, she said as she helped him carry the boat to the sea.

'No sooner had he started rowing than he felt the strange listlessness that he'd lived with for so long leaving him, and he felt his old strength coming back to him; and his old thoughts came back too, only this time the picture of Bleaval was crisp and clear in his mind, and he could almost feel the shower that he imagined to be sweeping across it at that very moment. He had always been a rower in a thousand, but that day he rowed with a strength that he had never imagined himself capable of, and in no time at all they were at the reef at the mouth of the bay.

'*This is where you turn back*, his companion said, smiling, but she didn't know about the charmed knife in his pocket nor the wise old woman's spell. *There's no turning back*, he said. *Not ever again!* And with that the coracle burst out of the bay past the reef and into the open sea which was ruffled with the kind of breeze that Neil hadn't felt on his face for as long as he could remember. And the fact that it was on his face, of course, meant that it was helping him on his journey. He didn't even notice that, for the first time since he had met her, there were tears in the eyes of the woman. And if he didn't notice them immediately there was no chance that he would notice them again, because she lifted the shawl from round her shoulders and buried her face in it. He was so busy with his rowing that he didn't notice her shoulders heaving as she sobbed.

'Nobody knows how long he rowed, but at last he made landfall and it was a beautiful evening just as it had been when he had been fishing for the cod and the lythe and the ling. The sea was flat calm, and he was in the hurry of a man at last in sight of home; he didn't even bother to go round the Blue Skerry to the Red Geo. He just let the boat ride the unbroken waves and beached her in the corner that you know – just where the sandy beach ends and the rocky shore begins. He hailed a man who was standing on the edge of the shore, and the man came down to look at him in wonder – looking at the stranger who had come out of the sea. And Neil couldn't believe that his eyes were seeing a stranger because from his boyhood he had known everybody who lived on that coast.

'*Who are you?* Neil asked in astonishment.

'*Who are you?* said the man on the shore, answering a

question with a question. *Who are you that comes out of the sea with the strange old woman?*

Neil turned round to look at his wife, and he felt the marrow draining from his bones. She had removed her shawl from her face and there, instead of the beautiful companion he had spent the unknown years with, was an ancient woman with a shrunken face and lines on it that could have been carved with a rusty knife. *Turn back while there is time,* she croaked. *Once before I gave you advice that you didn't take. In the name of all the spirits above and below the ocean take the advice that I'm giving you now. Turn your back to this shore of mortals and row with a mortal's strength while there is time. And let us get back to the land under the waves – to the land of the ever-young where my beauty will be restored to me; where we'll be young together in eternal sunshine. It is not often that a mortal is given a second chance of a happiness that he spurned. Turn back.*

'Neil looked sadly at Bleaval, and then at the frail-looking man standing at the sea's edge, and without another word he pushed his coracle back into the water. And the wind that had been in the west turned to the east and carried them both away out over the horizon. And the man on the shore stood looking after them in wonderment as they disappeared, and away at the back of his mind there stirred a story he had heard long ago about a man called Neil-who-was-lost.'

I had listened spell-bound. My father had always been a superb story teller, but it had been a long time since we had been close enough for him to tell me a story like that. Up there on the shoulder of Bleaval time had held its breath. My father laughed.

'I know what you're going to ask. You're going to use your clever brain and wonder how the story can be known if Neil-who-was-lost was really lost to another world. Well, one thing I'm going to tell you is that my grandfather, the Cleric, told me the story sitting here, or hereabouts, and he would have it that the man standing at the sea's edge was his own great-great-grandfather on his mother's side, and who was I to doubt him. And the other thing I'm going to tell you is that that story exists in one form or another in all sorts of parts of the world. Even the old Greeks had it, and they called their *land*

under the waves Atlantis. But we have as good a claim to it as
the Greeks ever had, because, if you look out there, you'll see
St Kilda and the Flannan Isles on the horizon; and if the old
Cleric was wrong when he told me that they are the tips of the
mountains of that drowned land, then I'm only passing on to
you a yarn that was passed on to me. But the funny thing is that
men laugh at our Highland version of the story, but they call
the Greek version a classic. That's the way of the world.'

From the top of Bleaval there came a whistle, signalling that
the man with the hole in his cheek had reached the summit
with his two good dogs and that the time had come to start
driving the sheep down to the plain. My father got up and
stretched himself, and felt for his pipe.

'You don't believe that story, do you?'

'No, of course I don't believe it, but –'

'Aye,' he said. 'That's always the way of it with boys when
they reach your age. But I always think that a boy loses a lot
when he learns to disbelieve.'

Chapter Five

The men of the village were mild of manner and moderate of language and, in the normal course of events, their most heated discussions would not have brought down the wrath of God on a vicarage. But on a sheep day it was different. It was as if the floodgates had been opened on the pent-up imprecations of frustrated weeks, and if the docile collies had been sensitive to the aspersions being hurled at the characters of themselves and their ancestors they would have leapt to follow the Gadarene swine. Instead, they slunk and stalked, and raced and froze, each with an inimical eye on his charges and a devoted one on his master. Unlike their owners the dogs worked silently, and for the first part of the drive the only sound was blasphemy. Then, slowly, the sheep began to raise echo; first the lambs in fear and then their mothers in reassurance. The older ones had been through it all before and, with a little encouragement, would probably have made their ways down to the fank in silent order; but the half-grown lambs were frightened and only the bravest of them would make a momentary stand and then, routed and embarrassed, would dive below his mother for a comforting teat, thumping her rear end up off the ground before being butted aside. Occasionally a seasoned old crock would glare defiance at a dog and thump her foreleg in challenge, and even the boldest dog would hang back for a moment till a skirl of Gaelic invective made him dart into the attack afresh.

My job, and that of the other young boys, was to mop up – to follow closely behind the dogs and search the scars and clefts in which wily old ewes and rams might have gone to ground in the hope of escaping the drive; although the principle aim of the August fank was to separate the lambs and forever wean them from their mothers, it was also in itself a 'cleaning up' operation designed to pull in beasts that had escaped shearing in the summer fanks, and lambs that had missed marking, or males that had been too young to castrate. It was also the fank at which farrow ewes and wethers would be taken to the croft and fattened for butchering at the beginning of winter. The drive had all the atmosphere of a cowboy round-up (sans horses) with whooping and shouting and the protest of the animals becoming more and more of a raucous chorus as they tightened into a semi-circle as we got nearer the fank by the shore. The fank itself was a large corral built of corrugated iron sheeting, showing patches of rust after ten years, with one big assembly area to receive the entire flock as it came off the hill, and with several smaller pens leading off it so that the sheep could be divided into their various categories and according to the various treatments being meted out to them. In my father's case, last year's crop would have his J brand burnt into their horns; young lambs overlooked in June would have their ears slit into his particular marking; all his beasts would have the blue spot of keel and the saddle-stripe of red renewed on the nape of their necks and on their backs respectively. There was a full day's work ahead, but, first of all, as the seven hundred sheep milled around the entrance there was much halloo-ing and beating of walking-sticks on the ground and frenzied barking as the dogs (who had worked silently till now) were given rein to use any method short of biting to coax a reluctant leader through the entrance of the main pen. Once one led the way, the rest – like the proverbial sheep – followed docilely.

Then, at last, time for the regaining of breath and the parcelling out of food. Sometimes, at that stage, the men would go home for a meal in order to give the sheep time to settle, but on that particular morning of sunshine there was plenty of left-over food from the Moderator's soiree and everybody sat on the rim of the shore for a picnic. It was one of the best-humoured fanks I could remember; there was a lot to talk about from the previous day – serious discussion and banter and a swopping of embellished yarns. The arrival of the drove had been seen from the village and various people who had not been on the hill themselves now drifted along either for the relaxation of a day out or to render extra assistance. One of them was Old Hector, and I was chagrined that he sat down at the far side of the group from me so that I couldn't satisfy my curiosity as to what (if anything) the mail-van had brought him. It was a dour-faced Geordie MacLellan who sat down without acknowledging the sarcastic salutations from left and right.

Once the business of the day got started there was no way in which I could button-hole Hector, but I did manage to mutter a hasty, 'Did the postman have anything?' as we brushed past one another, each of us astride a sheep being taken for belated clipping; it made my frustration worse to have him mutter a surly, 'Yes' out of the corner of his mouth just as somebody came to his rescue; manhandling a sheep is not a ploy for a man with gammy legs. I resigned myself to having to wait until the afternoon, when the most hectic part of the day's work would be easing off. But by the time that moment came Old Hector had been dispatched on one of the more unusual missions of his life.

When I referred to the moderation of the language of the crofters I exempted Tom-of-the-oaths because, at that time, he wasn't a resident of the village. I say resident, as opposed to native, because Tom-of-the-oaths was as native to the village as the crotal on the rocks. He was descended from a long and honourable line of people who had, for one reason or another, escaped the successive waves of evictions, but Tom himself had never settled down in the community because he had decided early on to become a professional shepherd and he had spent his life taking employment wherever it was offered to him. Occasionally it would be with a big farmer on the mainland; usually he found himself exiled to a hermit existence as keeper of the flock on one of the large, grassy, empty off-shore islands like Pabbay or Ensay or Kellegray – islands which had once been the homes of thriving populations but which had been emptied to make way for sheep-runs and had never been repopulated. It must have been on the mainland that Tom-of-the-oaths picked up his vocabulary, and it must have been in the loneliness of winters on the islands that he practised it. He had words that were unknown in our parts, but you could tell by the texture of them that they were potent curse-words; sometimes he stiffened them up even further by marrying them with four-letter English words with a cavalier illiteracy which rendered them all the more pungent; occasionally he melded them with our milder indigenous swear-words in a mutilating graft which could be awe-inspiring. 'I can't help you hearing Tom-of-the oaths,' my father used to say. 'But by God I can stop you from quoting him even if I have to leave the marks of my five fingers on your bare backside!'

His language was the only bad thing about Tom. In all other respects he was the kindliest and the gentlest of men; he was descended from one of the best poets that our island had ever produced and he could sing with a mellifluous voice not only his ancestor's songs but a vast anthology of the songs of the Hebrides. But shepherding was the love of his life, and although the great singing shepherd of the Old Testament would probably have disowned him as a fellow craftsman, Tom-of-the oaths had the cleaner conscience in the pursuits of the flesh. Otherwise I don't think my Great Aunt Rachel's sister would have married him when they were both rich in years.

Because shepherding was his hobby as much as his profession he attended every fank within travelling distance with the same sort of enthusiasm which some of his compatriots bestowed on revivalist meetings, and which modern aficionados confer on tennis tournaments. But it wasn't just as a spectator that he attended; he lent his skills wherever they were required, and his advice was as valuable as a vet's. In fact it was in an elementary veterinary capacity that he was most in demand. In those days there were no newfangled methods of castrating male lambs, nor any official practitioner to perform a task which had to be done unless the whole business of sheep-rearing was to dissolve into chaos since the balances of males to females was totally disproportionate in a species disinclined to monogamy. The common way of castrating was for the owner of a young ram to hold the beast to his chest with the corresponding rear and forelegs firmly pinioned while the operator swiftly sliced off the top of the lamb's scrotum, pressed out one testicle till he could grip it with his teeth and swiftly and smoothly pull it out, spit it away, and then do the same with other. The whole business took less than half a minute and, strange as it may seem, the lamb bounded free and in seconds was frolicking with his fellow, unaware and, apparently, unwounded. It was not a job which many men relished doing, because of the associations, psychological and otherwise; but to Tom-of-the-oaths it was all in the day's work and, for that reason even if for no other, his presence was always appreciated at the summer fanks.

Part of the 'mopping up' aspect of the August fank was the dealing with the occasional lamb who had escaped the knife in June which was when most of the budding rams were turned into wethers. That year, a couple of ours had had a reprieve and fate had only now caught up with them. My father had pointed them out to me and made it my responsibility to catch them and hold them for Tom-of-the-oaths when he became available. It's a job which I would find repellent now – even if it weren't prohibited by law in favour of an even more barbarous practice – but the country boy is introduced early to the work of men, and the less appealing aspects of farming and shepherding don't even register on his consciousness far less scar his psyche.

I was holding the second lamb for Tom and he had already spat out the first testicle. He had just extracted the second one, slowly and carefully, and was still holding it in his teeth when there was a sudden loud metallic click to the side of us. I flinced and Tom froze. Had his mouth fallen open in surprise it might have been better, but it hadn't; and before he could react in any way there was another click just as I turned round to see the second of two elegant, Pringled, lipsticked ladies lowering her camera while her companion stared at us in smiling fascination.

It all happened so quickly that I didn't see what Tom did with the testicle; his back was already turned to me as I bent down to release the lamb, who bounded off as if he had

71

enjoyed his moment of stardom; I was trapped, frozen where I stood.

'May I ask what you were doing with the little lamb?' asked the taller of the two ladies, in a voice tinged with smiling curiosity, and an accent redolent of Roedean. I stared at her. And even if I'd been a native English speaker I don't think I could have dreamt up a reply. Without a hint of graciousness I turned on my heel and ran over to my father. But Tom-of-the-oaths had got there ahead of me.

'I don't give a bugger what you do, but you better bloody well do something. It was your God-damned lamb, and if you think I'm going to have my picture splattered all over the *Sunday Post* with his ball hanging from my teeth you better bloody well start thinking again, John son of Finlay!'

My father knew better than to laugh because the shepherd had been known to use his fists with a dram in him, and he had worse than a dram in him now. He had embarrassment and cold fury – and an imagination so inflamed that he could impute to the homely *Sunday Post* actions which, if they were even contemplated, would have resulted in the sort of Press upheaval which was unheard of in those days, even on Fleet Street.

'Just calm down, Tom,' my father said. 'I'll talk to them and I'll send them home to Katie to see some spinning; that usually interests them and, with luck, Katie might be able to keep them occupied till I get home. We'll think of something. Or it will be the *News of the World* for sure –'

He moved off before Tom could conjure up even a swear-word and, a few moments later, he was deep in conversation with the two posh tourists. Somebody, unaware of what was going on, called on me to fetch a half-clad rogue sheep so that he could divest her of the tattered remains of her fleece, and by the time I looked again the two ladies were walking away from the fank chaperoned by Old Hector. I hoped that he could steer the conversation to Singapore, and at the same time felt annoyed that I would now have to wait till evening to find out what news Calum the Post had brought. Deep down I felt moderately certain that the tongue-tied bachelor Hector was not going to get himself involved in any conversation even remotely involving the objects of the ladies' inquisitiveness!

Two hours later the fank was over. All the odd jobs had been done, and the main job of the day was on the point of being accomplished. All the lambs were segregated in one pen with the mothers in another. In a few minutes a man with two good dogs would drive the older sheep on to the lower moorland, and when the in-bye gate was securely fastened on them the lambs would be herded on to the machair (the golf course as it was now) and they would be equally securely impounded. They would cry despairingly for a night and a day, but would fall silent as the replies from the moor became fewer and fainter.

Normally, on the day of a fank, my father would swallow a cup of tea and stretch out for an hour on St Clement's bench in the living room before settling down to a proper meal, such would be his tiredness. But today I could see him squaring his shoulders as he walked up to the house from the gate, and switching on a smile as he opened the door. He had been unusually pre-occupied on his way home, and had snapped my head off when I asked him what he thought the tourists would do with their photographs of Tom-of-the-oaths.

'What do you mean – photographs? It was only one picture they took.'

'No. They took two anyway; maybe more.'

'O God, it's a bloody film show they'll be having!'

I thought to myself that his own vocabulary was rivalling Tom's but I felt it wiser to make no comment.

There was no sign of his asperity as he entered the living room where the two ladies were sitting primly on St Clement's bench, balancing empty cups and saucers on empty plates.

'Ah, there you are ladies; I see you've been sampling the wife's tea … and her spinning too, by the looks of things!'

He glanced in my mother's direction, where she was sitting looking slightly flustered behind her wheel trying to unravel a tangle of thick thread from the hooks on the sheckle. Around her feet on the floor was enough mangled wool to make a cardigan. 'O, the ladies have been doing very well,' she said, adding with a slight glint of malice, 'I've been telling them that you would give them a few lessons on the loom when you came home.' The look in her eye meant 'that'll teach you to land your fancy visitors on me!'

'O that *would* be marvellous,' cooed the one who blushed.

73

'And then we'll be able to say that we've seen the whole Harris Tweed process from sheep to wearer –'

'The round-up was so fascinating,' the other one chipped in slightly apologetically. 'And the gentleman who escorted us here has had such an interesting life. He must find island life very quiet after the Far East.'

I wondered what legends of the Orient Old Hector had conjured out of one voyage to Singapore.

'Just a pity we didn't get a few more photographs, but Mr MacGeekan was convinced there was going to be a thunder-storm; I'm so glad he was wrong.'

My father hadn't sat down, and I could sense my mother daring him to do so. I knew that, at a conservative estimate, the visitors had been with her for two hours, and two hours with two enthusiastic English women in search of the Hebridean ethos could be an unnerving experience. The bare top of the stove was proof that she hadn't even been able to begin preparing the evening meal.

'Would you ladies like to have a go at the loom, then?' asked the man who wouldn't normally have looked at the loom for two days after a fank. With much oohing and fluttering they confirmed that they would. I had seen the routine many times before but, this time, I felt that I couldn't miss it and I slipped out to the weaving shed with them before my mother could dragoon me into dish washing or potato scrubbing. My three brothers were huddled on the red kist at the end of the table and two of them were old enough to take a share of the chores. I could almost hear my father's joints protesting as he eased himself on the hard wooden board which was his seat for the loom. While he was doing so the ladies were deciding that there was enough light to take a photograph if my father were to leave the door open – which, of course, he would.

There was nothing new about his performance except that it lacked a little of his usual energy. He pedalled his four pedals, swung the weaver's beam, shot the shuttle backwards and forwards through the meshing warp with deceptive ease. But his commentary lacked its customary sparkle and embellishment and he had woven a mere half yard when he stopped.

'Right then, which of you two ladies is going to have the first go; you look to me as if you had the legs and the arms of born

74

weavers.' He slipped off the wooden seat and surreptitiously winked at me but I couldn't for the life of me see why.

With giggles and protest and 'you go first, Madge' the tourists sorted themselves out and the one who blushed and was Madge pushed Susan onto the driving seat. After she had discovered that she could keep her skirt down over her knees *and* reach the pedals with her toes Susan attacked the loom with an abandon that would have qualified her for St Trinian's. As usual, with novices, the shuttle slithered over the top of the warp and not through it, but with such force that it left the beam altogether and if I hadn't jumped smartly aside I'd have suffered the fate of the photographed lamb.

'O dear! I've done something wrong, haven't I?'

'O Susan, you're far too impatient; didn't you notice that Mr Macdonald always had that wooden thing pushed away from him before he yanked the string?' Making allowance for her uncertain terminology, Madge did have a point and my father concurred as he retrieved the shuttle from the floor. He replaced it in the box nearer him, told Susan to push the beam away from her as far as she could (which she did, almost dislocating her pelvis), press her right foot down hard (which she did, and to her obvious astonishment the warp opened), jerk 'the string' to her right (which she did and the shuttle slid almost to the far end), pull the beam (which she did with a gasp) and, lo and behold, she had woven one thread at a speed which indicated that, if she maintained it, she might complete a full length of Harris Tweed by the time she attained the old age pension.

My father then had an inspiration. Why didn't Madge go and stand at the far side of the loom and look as if she were giving Susan a hint about her technique and he would take a photograph of them both so that they could prove to their friends in the deep south that they had, indeed, themselves woven a bit of the tweed they were going to buy – er – that is, of course, if they were going to buy it; something they were under no obligation whatsoever to do; the words had just slipped out. The two ladies weren't as soft as their giggliness indicated. They ignored the suggestion about buying, but they were most enthusiastic about the photograph and Madge slipped her camera off her shoulder before she took up a carefully studied pose at the other side of the loom. My father studied the camera and assured them that he had used the type before; which was news to me, because in no way did it resemble the ancient Box Brownie that my mother produced from the red kist once every summer. Just as he was on the point of raising it to his eye his finger appeared to slip and the back of the camera swung open.

'O Lord! I'm an idiot. What have I done? Have I ruined the film?'

His distress was such that the ladies recovered quickly from their initial flashes of annoyance; Susan slipped off the seat and Madge darted round from behind the loom to put him at his ease. It was nothing. It didn't matter. There were only three pictures on it – the ones taken at the 'round-up' – and they'd be bound to see another 'round-up' before they left the island. Of course, my father couldn't pay for the film; it was nice of him to suggest it; but, really and truly, it didn't matter. They had plenty of spools back in the hotel. After that my father relaxed, and, having saved the honour of Tom-of-the-oaths, decided to retrieve some of his own by giving Madge and Susan a long and good-humoured lesson in the art of weaving. They were surprisingly apt pupils, and once they got over their initial coyness each developed a remarkably determined set to her jaw and by the time they decided to set off for their hotel, although they had by no means mastered the art of weaving, they had mastered the theory of it. They called a cheery farewell to my mother as they made their ways down to the gate, escorted by my father, and they took a careful note of his address before they parted company with him.

'Well I'm dashed!' he was to say later when he got a letter requesting samples of Harris Tweed from a well-known London fashion house which listed among its directors two women whose first names were Madge and Susan. They were to remain good customers of his for a long time to come. But that was in the future. His immediate concern was to get down to the dinner which we could both smell as we reached the door.

'What on earth do you suppose Old Hector's up to?' my mother asked as we were half-way through the meal and had exhausted speculation about Madge and Susan.

'What do you mean?' I asked before my father could respond.

'The post arrived when I was milking his cow this morning. You know Calum the Post isn't such a bad character; he'll make us walk to the van to collect our mail but he got out today and walked the whole way up the hill to hand over Hector's letter to him. And that was just pure kindliness out of sympathy for the poor man's legs!'

'Pure curiosity more likely,' my father grunted. 'And I don't blame him in Hector's case; I don't suppose the old fellow's had a letter since Christmas. If Calum was doing his job he'd be walking up to every door with the letters as he would do if he worked in town. And what's more he wouldn't have a van if he were in town; he'd be tramping the streets with a big heavy sack on his back. He gets away with blue murder because he gives us lifts from time to time and brings the occasional box of groceries from Obbe!'

I couldn't care less about the postman's peccadilloes; I was dying to get up to Old Hector's but I knew I'd get my head in my hands if I suggested leaving the table before the rest were finished. And now that the strain of the tourists was off her shoulders my mother seemed determined to relax and let the evening slip by her.

'But you should have seen Hector. He got all flustered and excited, and dashed off to the end room with this large brown envelope as soon as Calum's back was turned. I think he was going to hide it; he certainly didn't have time to read the shortest of letters before he returned, and he couldn't wait to get me out of the house!'

'Perhaps he was getting some of those things they advertise under plain sealed wrappers.'

'John!'

I kept my face straight, pretending I didn't know what they were talking about.

'Anyway,' my mother went on, 'I'll have to milk Primrose tonight and tomorrow; Finlay's going to have other business on his hands.' She got up from the table and went across to the mantelpiece.

I had dropped out of the conversation because I had noticed that she kept referring to Old Hector as having received one

77

letter; in my imaginings I had come to believe that he would get a score at least. It took a second for her remark to register with me.

'What are you talking about, mammy? I'm going to milk Hector's cow as usual.'

'You're going to the doctor,' my brother burbled. 'You're going to Rodel to the doctor.'

'What's going on?' My father was as puzzled as I was.

My mother came back to the table with an official-looking brown letter in her hand. 'This came in the post today. Calum had to walk up to *this* house for once, because there was no-one here to meet him at the gate; he didn't know that I was to be in Hector's house or he'd have given it to me there. It's a letter from the Education Authority about your bursary for High School. You're to get a medical examination before you can register in Tarbert.'

'Right enough, we should have remembered that,' my father said, taking the letter from her. 'Jamie MacInnes had to have one; it's just a matter of form to make sure you haven't got T.B. or anything. You've got nothing to worry about on that score.' Tuberculosis was still endemic in the islands and every parent's dread was of 'that wee cough'.

'But what's that got to do with my milking Hector's cow?' I asked, trying to keep the exasperation out of my voice.

'I'll tell you what it's got to do with it.' My mother, for once, was carrying the burden of the argument; my father was studying the letter from Inverness. 'I've arranged with Geordie MacLellan to give you a lift to Rodel to the doctor tomorrow; he's got to collect some people at the hotel. And, if the doctor sees you right away you'll be able to get the bus back home at three o'clock –'

'I still don't see –'

'Will you keep quiet and stop interrupting me. You'll take the tin bath in from the end of the house and give yourself a good bath tonight; I'm not going to have you going to the doctor smelling of sheep and Hector's cow. What's all the excitement about Hector's cow anyway? You spend half your days grumbling about having to milk her; this is your chance to have the 'night off' that you keep pleading for – and a chance to have a good bath into the bargain! So I don't want to hear

78

any more about it. Your father will keep me company up and down past the cemetery and maybe he can satisfy his curiosity about Hector's letter while he's up there.'

She got up from the table. 'I'll have to milk our own cows before I do Hector's; and I'll have to get the young ones to bed before I do anything else. You two boys can do the dishes.'

'There's nothing to this,' my father said, putting the letter back in its envelope. 'The doctor will just sound your chest and test your eyes – that's all. You put two big pans on the stove for hot water for yourself; I'm going to have a smoke.'

I was seething with anger and frustration, but I knew that there was no point in protesting further. At this rate I'm going to be away to High School before I know Hector's fate, I thought sulkily to myself as I began to haul in water from the river. Normally I would have jumped at the chance of a trip to Rodel on my own, but this was not a normal occasion. It was infuriating to be able to see Old Hector's light shining yellow on the hillside – he must have lit his lamp early in expectation of my visit – and be as incommunicado as if I were a hundred miles away. I couldn't even have a smoke because all my douts were in Hector's house. But I'd have given up smoking just to know what that brown envelope contained.

Chapter Six

I was bathed and clean and sulky when my parents returned from milking Hector's cow, and I had the mildest trace of an irritating giddiness which, I was to learn in years to come, was already the beginning of nicotine craving. Over the past six months or so hardly a day had passed without my having smoked at least one cigarette, and since the beginning of the summer holidays I'd had at least one after each morning milking and a couple as I relaxed with Hector after the evening chore. There was no suggestion of any of the much publicised diseases attributable to cigarette smoking nowadays but there was a vague unease that cigarettes might make one more susceptible to the 'wee cough'. Indeed many of the deaths which were put down to T.B. may well have been lung cancer although not diagnosed as such. But the simple fact was that, even at that early age, I was 'hooked', and on that particular day I had already missed out on my morning fix because of the fank. Niggling at my mind also was the thought that most of tomorrow would also be a smokeless day unless my parents decided to give me some spending money for my Rodel trip; Geordie MacLellan, with whom I was going to travel, was a smoker himself but he couldn't be trusted to keep my vice secret because he had boys of his own and, consequently, parental attitudes!

'How did you get on?' A slight fleeting frown on my mother's face showed that she had detected the surliness in my voice, but she decided to let it pass.

'Fine,' she said. 'Why not? I've milked a cow before. But I thought I was never going to get home once your father and Old Hector started blethering; I thought fanks were tiring affairs, but apparently they're only exhausting as far as doing work around the croft is concerned. When did Donald go to bed?'

My father saved me from having to tell a lie rather than admit that my younger brother had slipped off only when he heard the gate squeak.

'What's going on between Old Hector and yourself?' he asked. 'He barely thanked your mother for doing the milking for him, and you'd have thought somebody had stolen his last ha'penny when he heard that you wouldn't be going up in the morning either. Are the two of you plotting something? Although I can't imagine that –'

My mother cut in, saving me from replying. 'Loneliness,' she said. 'That's what it is. The poor man's going out of mind living on his own up on the hill there. Maggie may have given him a tonguing now and again but at least it was the sound of a human voice. And that house of his is becoming a real piggery. I offered to wash down the dresser for him but he nearly took my head off when he saw me going to touch a plate!'

Good for Hector! If my mother had started cleaning the dishes on the dresser she'd have come across my packet of Woodbines and my hoard of douts, and she wouldn't have required the two sights to know who had stashed them there.

'Pity we couldn't get a wife for him,' said my father, yawning and reaching for the Bible. 'There's no way he's going to be able to hang on to Primrose once Finlay goes off to High School; there's a limit to how long the women of the village can keep on doing his milking for him once winter comes in. I don't know why the hell he wants a cow anyway. There's nothing wrong with nessels when you get used to it and it's a damn sight cheaper than a cow in the long run.' 'Nessels' was another word that had been adopted into Gaelic, regardless of whether or not the product had been produced by the famous Swiss firm; the other word that was creeping in was 'idal' for the version of tinned milk trade-named 'Ideal'.

My mother had come back down from the hill when big

Geordie drew up at the gate in the Armstrong. 'Now,' my father was instructing me, 'you'll do exactly as I say. Geordie will take you to the door of the bar and if he goes in for a pint himself he'll keep you right. But if he doesn't, you'll go in on your own even if you're not the age. There won't be many people there at that hour, and you'll be able to spot the doctor without any bother. He's tall and as bald as a baby's backside, and he'll be leaning against the far end of the bar with a pint at his elbow. You'll go up to him and explain what you want and hand him that form. He'll tell you the rest, and when he's filled in the form you'll hand him that half crown and tell him that your father wants him to have a dram. Understand?'

I nodded and took the half crown and the envelope containing the Education Committee form.

'And there's a half crown for yourself. The bus will cost you sixpence, and that means you can spend two shillings in the shop. Don't spend it all on sweets or your mother will kill me; get a couple of pencils or something, and bring back a bar of toffee for Donald.' Geordie's klaxon sounded impatiently. 'Off with you or Geordie'll be away without you! And don't lose that form whatever you do ...'

Fine! I was rich. Eight pence would buy twenty Red Label Woodbine which were newly on the market, and the cheapest by far, and a box of matches would be a ha'penny. I'd have enough left over for a token pencil and a bar of toffee for Donald forbye.

My father's instructions with regard to the doctor may sound bizarre to today's reader, but they were no more so than the haphazard medical system which prevailed in parts of the West Highlands at that time. Although the Southlands had now been completely repopulated for three or four years, we still didn't have a permanent doctor of our own. Not that he was necessary; the District Nurse and the old wives who were skilful in the arts of midwifery normally fulfilled the needs of the district and a doctor was rarely summoned except in cases of serious accident and for the signing of death certificates and the filling in of rare official documents like my own. The result was that the series of locums who processed through the Southlands while the authorities were debating the need for a full-time doctor, tended to be people who, by being exiled to us from the main, were suffering a fate second only to being struck off the medical register, gentlemen who were fanatical anglers, or, occasionally, newly qualified men fired with Hippocratic enthusiasm. Whichever category they belonged to, they found themselves with more time on their hands than they had hitherto imagined to exist, and if they weren't careful they found themselves fighting an increasingly difficult battle against alcoholism. Most of them decided to escape in the nick of time. Dr Frankinson, the present incumbent, had decided to surrender.

He was an extremely popular man, and a marvellous raconteur. When he had money he was extremely generous in the bar; when he hadn't, his position in society afforded him a length of 'slate' which the proprietor would never have allowed a local. For many years now, the Rodel Hotel has been presided over by one of the great characters of the West Highlands – a Hebridean with a personality which would have taken him to the top in any profession, and a heart of gold; not the least of his qualities is that he treats all men the same, except the less able, whom he treats even better. But his predecessor was in a different mould, and tended to touch his cap to 'society', and since the doctor fell into that category he was able to use the hotel as his club. Dr Frankinson went one better – during his short stay he used the bar as his surgery as well! And that was where I found him when my eyes got used to the gloom after the August sunshine. He was standing exactly as my father had described – bald and impressive, and elegant in a well cut tweed suit which was so worn that only a member of the aristocracy or a millionaire would have been seen dead in it.

'Well laddie,' he said, in a rich rolling mainland accent. 'You've got the look of a man looking for the doctor. But it's not for yourself – that's for sure – you're as healthy as a stirk. Who is it that thinks he's dying? Tell him he'll get better, and if not he'll be better off!' The twinkle in his eye took any suggestion of heartlessness out of his talk.

'It's nobody,' I said, shoving the envelope with my form at him. 'It's the form for High School; I've got to have it signed by a doctor.'

'Ah! One of those.' He studied the form for a while. 'So

you're off to High School, eh? And what are you going to do with all the fine education you'll collect there? A minister, eh? Or a schoolmaster? Or a damn fool doctor like me?'

'A banker,' I said. It wasn't a subject to which I'd given much thought of late. I'd had vague notions of writing for newspapers at one time, but most people to whom I'd mentioned it had dismissed it as flim-flam. A secure job with a salary and a pension was the thing to go for; 'a schoolmaster in the city' – now there was something to aim for. But recently a second cousin of mine had got himself a job in the bank in Tarbert without having had to go through the whole hassle of a University degree, and from his very first day he was never seen in old clothes again, and in no time he had acquired a spanking new motor bicycle. Everybody maintained that he 'wouldn't be stuck in Tarbert for long; that he would get on in the bank and get away'. The 'getting away' idea had been deeply instilled in me from my earliest days in school, and the bank seemed to offer a shorter cut than either the ministry or teaching.

'A banker! Don't be daft. Only little Hitlers want to be bankers and bank managers; they want to sit behind big desks and bully people like me who are better at subtraction than at multiplication!' I hadn't the faintest idea what he was talking about; I hadn't learn't to recognise the symptoms of an overdraft.

'You go and get yourself a good education and come back here and take over your old man's croft. He's no damn good as a crofter; I don't know what put the idea into his head. He should have been in parliament, or writing poetry, or some-thing daft like that.'

'Do you know my father?'

''Course I do. We were in the army together. He wouldn't mention that, of course. Lucky John, we used to call him – well, we were both lucky I guess. Tell him I'll be up to see him one of those days. But you come back home when you get your education and take over the croft!'

I was dying to ask him more about the army and my father's part in it, but I could sense that he had deliberately put a full stop to that part of the conversation.

'But I wouldn't need to go away to school to do that,' I

ventured. 'You don't need education to be a crofter.'

'And what bloody fool told you that? Not your father, that's for sure. Education isn't for *being* something, boy; education is for enjoying whatever you are. The only thing you have to *be* in life is yourself. There are only two ways to enjoy yourself – one is to have a good education so that you can understand how much worse off you could be; the other way is to have no education at all, and not be discontented with your lot in the first place. Bloody banker! Huh! If I thought that's what you'd become I'd give you a medical certificate that wouldn't get you anywhere except into a hospital. Come here!'

He led the way out into the back yard where the empty beer barrels were stacked and he smoothed out the medical form on the top of one. He produced a fountain pen and filled it in from top to bottom without glancing once at me or asking one single question. 'There you are,' he said when he had signed his name with a flourish; 'that'll see you right. Nobody will ever read the damn thing anyway – they're just a lot of little Hitlers there, in Inverness – just like bankers, bossing people around!' He handed me the form and was turning away when I remembered the half crown.

'My father said to give you that; he said you were to have a dram.'

He smiled. 'Is that what he said? Well, you tell him from me that that doesn't cover what he owes me for the last job I did for him!' He took the half crown and put it in his pocket, and solemnly handed me back two shillings. 'You don't have to mention any other sums of money,' he winked. 'Just tell him I took the half crown and that way you won't be telling a word of a lie!'

'But –'

'Only goats and rams butt!' He turned on his heel but stopped again. 'Are you going home on the bus?'

'Yes.'

'Then you've got two hours to spare. See that road there? Go up there till you come to a little cottage with a red roof on it. Knock on the door and tell them the doctor asked you to get the key to St Clement's, and when you get it go and spend an hour prowling there among your people's history; there's education for you.' He made to go and hesitated yet again. 'O,

85

by the way, I've put in your form that you've got a very slight weakness of the eyes, and that you'll soon be needing spectacles like your father.'

'My father hasn't got spectacles –'

'No. But he needs them. Otherwise he'd have noticed the yellow staining on the tips of the first two fingers of your right hand. If I didn't know better I'd have sworn it was nicotine – that's the English for the poison in cigarettes!' And with that he strode back into the bar. I stood looking after him for a moment, remembering some of the things I'd heard people say about him. 'Brilliant;' they used to say. 'He's a better doctor drunk than others are sober.' I was to get to know that for myself one day, when he came to save my life. But that was a long way ahead. I decided I'd take his advice and go to St Clement's; there would be time to get cigarettes later on. The morning craving had passed, and as I fingered the florin piece in my pocket alongside my other half crown I had the comforting thought that I could afford Capstan for once.

It was bitterly cold in St Clement's; the centuries old church hadn't absorbed enough of the summer heat to last it through the wet July that we'd had, and it wasn't responding to the paler sun of a Hebridean August. And it was dark, except where shafts of light cut through from the narrow windows. But it had an atmosphere that I had felt only once before, not in a church but on a lonely island in a moorland loch. Just inside the door I found a large wooden spatula with the church's story sketchily outlined on it, telling how it was the oldest cruciform church in the Western Isles, probably contemporary with Iona Abbey. That didn't mean very much to me, but I was transfixed in front of the tomb of Alasdair Crotach, the fierce chief of Clan Macleod who had rebuilt the church four hundred years ago and re-dedicated it to the patron saint of sea-farers. He had been a ruthless chief, Alasdair Crotach (called Alasdair Humpbacked because of a sword wound that had disfigured him), and yet he found it in his heart to re-build a great church and build for himself a tomb inside it. I stood staring at his effigy carved in stone, with his sword in his hand and his dogs at his feet, and felt the cold atmosphere around me disappearing. Dr Frankinson had been right; this was history, pulsing and living even although there couldn't be bones down there after four hundred years; the dust would have returned to dust – just as it would have done whether the man had been saint or sinner, and this, obviously from the potted history, had been both. The same tourist guide, on the wooden hand board, reminded me that, of course, St Clement's had been thatched in Alasdair Crotach's day – much in the same style, I thought, as Old Hector's house and the few other old black houses on the moor's edge. It had been Lady Dunmore in the nineteenth century (the laird's wife who had founded the Harris Tweed industry) who had rescued the church from ruin again, and had replaced the old thatch with slate. Generation after generation had made an effort to leave its own little notch of remembrance on a building which stood on a site of worship that was older than Christianity. I had begun to feel quite the young man as the days of High School were approaching; now, suddenly, I felt very young indeed.

Outside, I wandered around among the ancient tombstones – the railed sepulchres of landlords of vanity, craving for their immortality, and the once ornate monuments of grandeur looked tawdry beside the simple dignity of St Clement's. More dignified by far were the flat stones on which the simple inscriptions had long since faded; one of them, my guide notes told me, covered the grave of one of the great poets of the nineteenth century; another (nobody could be sure which) lay on the grave of one of the greatest bards of the whole Highlands – Mary MacLeod of the seventeenth century, whose songs live on as memorials more lasting than stone.

I went back inside the church again and climbed the narrow circular stairway built into the wall, and came out at the top. From there, the whole history fell into place. From there I could see why Rodel had been the Harris capital of the Macleods, who are, to this day the Macleods of Harris although their castle is in Skye. Down below me was the harbour, landlocked almost so that the chief's war galleys could find shelter from the worst storms and a defensible refuge from enemies. and just by turning left towards the east I could see Skye itself in the distance and I could tell that it wouldn't take a galley, under sail or under sixteen oars, long to link the chief's two strongholds – giving him virtual control of the Minch separating the Outer Hebrides from Skye and the mainland. My school books had taught me that history was something that happened elsewhere – in far away places like Lucknow and Cawnpore; in Omdurman and Khartoum; in Kimberley and Ladysmith ... the books had taught me that history had to be monumental to be important, and that the making of empire was history's chief end.

Yes, Dr Frankinson was right. But the sudden recollection of the doctor reminded me of his jibe about my nicotine-stained fingers, and that, in turn, reminded me that I had better hurry if I were to get to the shop in time to catch the bus. I left St Clement's behind me for thirty years ...

The woman in the shop looked at me as if she ought to know me, but, fortunately, she decided that she didn't and the sight of the silver in my palm allayed her qualms about selling cigarettes to somebody who was manifestly under age. When she handed me a flat twenty packet of Capstan I asked her for two packets of ten instead. She looked puzzled. 'Why do you want two packets? That'll cost you a shilling whereas you'll get a full twenty for eleven pence ha'penny leaving you a ha'penny for a box of matches.'

'They're for different people.' I said, marvelling at how glibly the lie came. But I couldn't explain to her that two packets of ten could be concealed, one in each trouser pocket, while a packet of twenty couldn't. Certainly a twenty pack would have looked manly and impressive but, unfortunately, this was one thing which I couldn't use to impress. The old lady looked relieved not to be breaking the law, and she went on happily to serve with me with slabs of toffee and a couple of pencils. I had made a mental calculation to be careful; Dr Frankinson had warned me not to tell that he had taken only sixpence for his consultation, so I had to be sure that such purchases as I could produce at home were no more than I could cover from the money my father had given me.

To my delight the bus was empty when I boarded it back at the hotel and, what was more, the driver was 'a trusty' – the hero of every youngster in the island. He was only in his early twenties and yet here he was heaving a long blue bus that could take thirty passengers round the island's hairpin bends day in and day out. And he did it with style too – appearing to lean with his bus like a racing driver and managing to give an appearance of dash and speed while keeping up a constant flow of racy anecdote.

'Have a fag,' I said nonchalantly, using yet another word that had become a fashionable Gaelic noun. 'I'll light it for you.' And to my delight he took it as if it were the most natural thing in the world for me to be offering it; it made me feel sixteen at least. We chatted about this and that as the bus threaded its way through gentle Rodel glen, with me hiding – under the most casual air – the fact that I was scanning the road ahead, ready to extinguish my cigarette if I saw an adult flagging down the bus. Meanwhile Jackie flung out of his driver's window a copy of the *Daily Express* here and a *Daily Record* there at the gates of those who had placed orders. And that was almost every gate, because the rumours of war were building up steadily as news filtered through of crisis meetings, and as Germany annexed more and more of Europe. Whenever I glanced behind me through the rear window of the bus I could see people trotting down their paths – people who had obviously been watching from their windows, waiting for their daily dose of news. Many of them had wireless sets by then, but the newspapers were more solid, somehow, and more credible than the disembodied voice from the box.

Rodel glen is the nearest to parkland that I know in the whole of the Hebrides. And not without reason. Its name in Gaelic means 'the choicest of dales' and it was for many years the home farm of the chief of MacLeod, and one of the last of their lands that the MacLeods parted with when their estates were sold off to meet debts in the eighteenth and nineteenth centuries. The petrified remains of dead forest still clung on to the hillside on our left as we drove north, and through the ghostly skeletal remains of trees from which the sap had departed, like the blood from old ladies' corpses, I could see a clearly etched ridge of green which looked like the manicured border of a huge path.

'Is that another road over there, Jackie?'

Jackie didn't have to look.

'Well, it is and it isn't. They tell me that was a drive-way once, and one passenger (I can't remember who it was) was saying that his grandmother could remember ladies driving along through the woods there in a carriage drawn by four horses. It must have been quite a sight. Lord Dunmore it must have been. They say that the night he died, though he was away from the island then, a mighty big thunderstorm broke out – just when his soul was passing on – and every one of the great trees died where it stood. Makes you think doesn't it?'

It made me think that Jackie was more of a poet than I had suspected, but a few moments later as we crested the hill above Obbe, I had reason to revert to my original assessment.

'Look at this bloody son-of-a-bitch here; he's going to bring that ram aboard the bus and I won't ever get a fare for it. All I'll get will be hell when the boss finds sheep shit all over the bus!'

Sure enough, there was a hefty crofter whom I knew by sight although I didn't know his name, standing with a massive ram at the road-side and, slightly self-consciously, flagging down the bus.

'Hello, Jackie. I'm sorry to bother you, but I missed the Board of Agriculture landry; the wife was saying that you wouldn't mind giving me a wee lift as far as Borve?'

'I don't mind giving you a wee lift for a wee fare, but I'll get my books if I take that bloody beast aboard! You know that perfectly well!'

'Indeed I do Jackie; it was just seeing you with your uncle's calf in the bus a couple of weeks ago that made me think the rules had, maybe, been softened a bit. But if you'd rather not –'

Considering the ram was already aboard, Jackie didn't have much option.

'I'll tell you one thing for sure – I'll be charging you a ticket for him then. A full ticket!'

'Dammit man,' said the crofter. 'Do you think I'd be scrounging him on for free; but the snag is I've only got my own fare neat, and I was just going to ask if you would get the office to send me a wee account?'

Jackie spluttered.

'How the hell can I get the office to send a wee account for something that's not supposed to be aboard anyway? Keep the bloody thing under control then,' he yelped as the ram attacked a seat with his massive head. And he slammed the bus into gear sending the crofter flying on top of his beast.

'A terribly hasty temper that fellow's got,' the new passenger said to me, shaking his head. 'He'll have an accident one of those days!' He sat down and lit his pipe, and Jackie drove on in silence.

As we reached the village I glanced up towards the hill and I could see Old Hector plowtering about at the end of his house. I toyed with the idea of getting off at his road end, but it was only four o'clock and I knew that my mother would be anxious for news of my visit to the doctor. Having waited so far, I could bide in patience for another few hours. Jackie pulled up at our gate and handed me my father's *Daily Express* as I fumbled for my sixpence.

'Ach forget it, boy; at least you don't shit in my bus!'

Running public service transport profitably in a close-knit community was a problem in the Hebrides in those days. And still is.

'How was Dr Frankinson?' asked my father as he prepared to settle down to his *Express*.

'Fine,' I said. 'He filled in the form.'

'And did he take the half crown?'

'Yes,' I said, with moderate truth. 'But he said to tell you it didn't cover what you owed him. What did he mean?'

'O!' He looked a little nonplussed, but he smiled as his hand wandered unconsciously to the scar on the top of his head – a scar which he always claimed was the result of an accident long ago. He checked his hand. 'I don't know,' he said, biting his lip. 'I don't know at all. He's got a funny sense of humour, has Fred.' And with that he lost himself in the paper. Whatever Dr Frankinson meant, I never found out; nor did I ever hear reference again from either of them to their having been together in the war.

My brother came charging in demanding to know whether I'd brought him his bar of toffee; my mother came in from feeding the chickens wanting to know whom I'd seen and how I'd got on. It was soon the hour for the evening meal, and, one way and another, the time passed till it was reasonable for me to suggest that I'd better go and milk Hector's cow.

'Aye, you'd better,' my mother said. 'I hope you get more thanks than I got. That man gets more crotchety every day; it's just as well there's nobody with him who has to put up with him!'

I wondered if that situation might not be on the point of changing. I would soon know.

Chapter Seven

Old Hector was standing outside his door shifting impatiently from foot to foot, which for him was a more cumbersome effort than for most. He didn't say anything as I arrived, panting from my jog up the hill; he waited till we were inside where there was no danger that his voice could carry down to the village over the August evening that was so still that a fleck of down would have fallen straight to earth. But when we did get inside he exploded. He was a mild-mannered man, as I've taken pains to establish, but I knew that he had a secret store of pungent vocabulary picked up on his only voyage. Now he unleashed it.

'You're a son-of-a-bitch, that's what you are – and an ungrateful one at that. For all these months I've plied you with cigarettes and kept your bad habits secret forbye. And what do you do to me? You blackmail me into trouble, and as soon as I'm in it up to my arse you start having baths and buggering off to Rodel. I'll tell you this – for two pins I'd have let your mother start "clean-springing" the house and let her find your filthy Woodbines hiding behind my best crockery –'

I made several attempts to check his rhetoric but I might as well have tried, single-handed, to stop a flock of sheep in stampede. At long last he began to run out of energy and he flopped down into the Taransay chair. I suspected that he was beginning to feel better.

'I know you had to go and see the doctor. I know you had to

have a bath because that's the sort of thing that fancy boys going off to High School have to get used to. Your mother told me all that; but even if you couldn't have milked the cow you could have found some way of slipping up here for two minutes when you must have known that I was getting a nervous break-down all alone on this bloody hill –'

At last I was able to jump into a pause as he took two breaths instead of one, and I tried to explain to him that there was no way that I could slip out of the house for the time I knew would be required without turning my parents' puzzlement into suspicion. And how, I asked him, would he have liked it if they had elicited some clue that would have allowed them to stumble on to his secret?

No – he wouldn't have liked that at all; of course he wouldn't. 'But you could have fixed it so that they wouldn't suspect. You were quick enough to find a way for yourself and Gillespie to get to James's wedding, and back home again, without your parents finding out! That was all very well; that was something *you* wanted to fix for that Gillespie and yourself, but when it came to doing something for poor old Hector it was too much trouble to put your brains to work –'

'How?' I spluttered and stopped! How on earth had he found out about that escapade of mine and Gillespie's all those years ago? I had forgotten about it myself. Gillespie and I covered our tracks so well that when we did, occasionally and accidentally, let slip some reference to the wedding feast that we had attended as invisible guests people had imagined that we were either telling lies or else creating fantasies out of bits and pieces of information that we had overheard. Yet here was Hector after all this time casually referring to the incident as if it had been common knowledge all the time. I had drifted away momentarily into a puzzled dwam and I'd lost track of Hector's ravings and rantings till one fragment of reproach scythed through my dismay '… but of course for all you cared those three women could have come charging up the hill in their Sunday hats and nothing else, and started fighting over me like crows over carrion –'

'*Three* women! What do you mean, *three* women? Did you get three replies?'

'Hah! I thought that would get through to the little bit of

conscience that you've got left. Yes, I got three replies. Isn't that what's been driving me into the crazy house? Wondering how I could barricade myself in if I saw the three of them hopping out of Mitchell's bus down at the road there. I'll tell you this – when I looked out of the window this morning and saw your mother coming up the hill with a scarf round her head I thought that my heart coming up would meet my porridge going down! What the hell are you laughing at?'

I couldn't tell him that it was the word 'hopping' that had kittled my fancy. Never in my most optimistic imaginings had I envisaged any potential candidate of an age and an agility that would permit her to *hop* off a three inch doorstep far less off Mitchell's tall bus. At best I had hoped for one desperate woman with at least one hand sufficiently free of rheumatism and arthritis to enable her to milk a cow; in fact, in all my thinking, the need for a milker for Primrose had rated higher than a bride for Hector, but my common sense told me that our only chance of securing the former was by procuring the latter.

'I wasn't laughing at you,' I assured him. 'I was laughing at the idea of you mistaking my mother for a woman who would reply to the advertisement. And in any case why can't you get it into your head that nobody's going to come chasing after you? No sane woman would climb on to Mitchell's bus and ask Jackie to take her to 427's house. You're only a number, so far!'

'Aye – a back number; and that's what I'm going to remain. If I were a drinking man I'd convince myself I'd have the excuse of having been drunk when I allowed you to talk me into this whole mad business. Just think of it – picking a woman from a list of applicants, as if you were picking a pair of boots from a catalogue! If those letters did nothing else they brought me to my senses.'

I hadn't wanted to push him towards the subject of the letters although I'd been dying to see them; but this was my cue. I pulled one of my packets of Capstan out of my pocket and lit a cigarette as casually as I could. I saw his eyes going to the crisp new packet of ten but he didn't say anything; instead he was reminded to light his own pipe.

'Are you not going to show me the letters, then?'

He waited till his pipe was glowing and then got up, shakily, and went over to the dresser. He rummaged deep into the back of a drawer, and it was obvious that he had hidden the letters so carefully that even he was having difficulty finding them. Finally he turned round with three rather grimy small envelopes in his hand; either the writers weren't unduly beset by cleanliness or Old Hector had spent the last two days thumbing them over and over again. I suspected that the latter was the more likely. He handed over the letters with a suggestion of embarrassment but, at least, he had recovered his equanimity for the time being. 'Poor souls,' he said. 'I wonder if any one of them would have written if she had a clue about what a poor bargain she was chasing; it would be a cruel joke if there was a chance of one of them ever finding out.'

I ignored the implication of his remark.

'My mother said it was one brown envelope you had received; that's why I was surprised when you mentioned *three* women.'

'O, your mother told you that did she? That's just what I mean about the danger of this whole thing becoming known in the village; I'd be a laughing stock for the rest of my born days. There are plenty of them think I've got a weakness in the head as it is. However, your mother was right; it was a brown envelope all those wee ones came in, but you don't think I was going to be daft enough to leave it lying around for anybody to see – addressed to me as plain as plain could be. Not on your life; I burnt it the moment your mother's back was turned.'

I began to wonder if he had a 'weakness in the head' after all: he had burnt a perfectly innocuous envelope with his name and address on it (an envelope which could have contained anything from a mail order catalogue to a copy of the Church of Scotland's *Life and Work*) but he had clung on to three white envelopes (or, to be precise, two white ones and a blue one) clearly addressed Box 427, Stornoway Gazette, Stornoway. It wouldn't have taken Dixon Hawke or The Saint long to conclude that Old Hector had been advertising for something.

Two of the letters were terse and to the point. The first one read, 'Dear Sir, regarding your advertissment for a wife in the Gazette I would be much obliged if you could send me more information. I am used to living on a croft. Please reply by return. Your obdt servant …'

The second one was in the same sort of vein. 'Dear Sir, i have been reading your advert. And i would like to say that i would like to offer myself if the conditions of employment is right, i am a respectfully unmarried woman not that i haven't had plenty of men after me but not yet one i would look at but I would like to see a fotograf or yourself. Your sincerely …'

Both those were from neighbouring Lewis and both approximately an hour and a half's bus journey away. The third one, in the blue envelope, was from one of the smaller off-shore islands which it is better, even now, to leave unidentified. 'Dear Mr 427,' it read, 'If you advertisement was a legpul it doesnt matter but if you are a nice man and serious I would like you to know that I am to. I will be fifty years of age next year and my life is very lonely sometimes. If you would like to meet me you are welcome to come and see me here but if it is your idea to make a fool of some poor woman then He who forgives all things will forgive that too. Yours faithfully …'

'I think this one from the island is the one,' I said. 'She's the only one who can make a reasonable attempt at spelling; and she sounds a good woman.'

He looked at me with the same sort of stunned expression as I'd seen on his face when I had suggested advertising in the first place, now almost a fortnight ago. He looked at me, glanced at his pipe, looked into my eyes again as if trying to detect some madness there; he gave a dry half laugh and automatically reached into his pocket for the piece of paper which he kept for spills for lighting his pipe. 'You're being serious,' he said. 'I thought I was the madman for agreeing with you when you had this crazy idea in the first place, but then I thought that you were pulling my leg and that I'd be a poor sport if I didn't go along with you. But now that you've landed me in this dung heap you really do think I'll go along with you. Well, I'll tell you my lad – the fun's over.' He bent down over the fire and got his pipe going; he then plucked the letters out of my hand. 'We'll just forget that this ever happened; just you go and milk Primrose and when you're finished come in and have a cigarette and we'll just yarn away like old times.'

'What about breach of promise?' I asked, casually, as I

turned to get the milking pail. 'It won't be one case you'll have to defend but three.'

Breach of promise was forever featuring in the popular papers of the day as one of the more lurid hazards of High Society, and even in the Scottish Highlands more than one fine fellow had trudged to the altar under threat.

'At least they can't take the house from you,' I said as I reached the door. 'But the best price that you can get for Primrose won't seem much when it's divided between three angry women.'

'Get out!' he said. But I noticed out of the corner of my eye that he didn't throw the three letters into the fire as I was fully expecting him to do. Instead he went over to the dresser where he was obviously going to restore them to their hiding place.

Primrose was twitching her tail impatiently as I reached her, and the firm chomp of her cud indicated that she wanted this whole tedious operation over and done with as quickly as possible so that she could get moving from under the attack of the midges. They were out for blood that night and I couldn't get a two handed rhythm into the milking because, every few moments, I had to disengage one hand and rub my face to get rid of the half-sting, half-itch, of the greatest August menace in the West Highlands. For once in my life I was grateful when Primrose switched her tail and caught me a wallop on the side of the face; normally it made me swear at her but tonight it was as if she were trying to protect us both. Over on the far edge of the moor I could see a cow which looked for all the world as if it had been fitted with a puffing chimney, and I knew that Gillespie's father was crouched in the same situation as myself but using a deterrent that wasn't available to me. I wished I could chance lighting up but I knew that if my mother or father happened to go to the river for a pail of water they would see the smoke rising just as I was seeing it rising from behind our neighbour's cow; and they would know for certain that Hector's pipe would never achieve such proximity to hoof or horns. That reminded me that Old Hector hadn't come near me since I'd started milking, and that meant that he wasn't interested in opening peace negotiations. Normally, after one of our tiffs, he found some excuse to come slinking to the dyke and he would launch on some conversation far removed from the point at issue. The fact that he didn't appear might well mean that his annoyance had been genuine. That made me begin to think seriously for the first time about the implications of what I had initiated. I had never in fact, I admitted to myself, decided whether I was having fun at Hector's expense or whether something had prompted me towards a genuine solution to a problem to which the old man (as I still considered him) was going to have to face up much sooner than he appreciated.

As I returned to the original pair of teats for the second round I found myself wondering if the idea of a 'plotted' marriage was such a crazy one after all. Even then I had begun to wonder if the great 'romantic' idea of love as an indispensible ingredient of marriage was such a valid idea after all; it seemed to me that the hardest headed, least lovey-dovey, business-like couples that I knew seemed to be faring a dashed sight better than the ones who clucked and petted and called each other 'my dear' even when they were arguing; and the *Royal Crown Reader, Book VI*, from which I had recently parted company, had a long chapter on the frightfully 'un-British' custom of arranged marriages in places like India. Nobody had arranged much for Hector hitherto; perhaps it was time somebody did.

I squeezed the last couple of squirts from Primrose, felt that her udder was as empty as a collapsed bagpipe, and whipped the fetter-rope from around her ankles. She lifted her legs into the air like a frisky calf and set off to wage her own private war with the midges. As I hurried back to the smokey shelter of Hector's house I could see that the demons were drowning themselves in their hundreds in the froth on the top of my milking pail; it was some slight consolation for a face that was beginning to feel swollen.

I decided that I'd had enough of badinage for a night and after I had strained the milk and set the basins I concealed my new consignment of cigarettes behind the plate on the dresser, and sat down to smoke two of the douts left over from two nights before.

'Do you remember that queer fellow who arrived at the Moderator's soiree by mistake?' Hector asked. And I knew by his tone that he was determined to move the conversation away from any controversial ground; I settled back in my chair, placing my second dout where I could reach it comfortably and, when the time came, re-light it from the stub end of the other in the sophisticated manner known as 'chain-smoking'.

'Yes, of course I remember him; nobody will ever forget him. I tried to ask Geordie MacLellan about him yesterday but he nearly took my head off. Why do you ask?'

Hector chuckled. 'O, yes. Big Geordie wouldn't want to talk about that fellow; he made Geordie take him all the way back to Stornoway for free and, what was worse, kept Geordie waiting at the Tarbert Hotel for an hour while he himself was knocking back whiskies with one of the Tarbert nobs. Never even invited Geordie in from the car. But listen to what I'm going to tell you. I saw Big Neil today and he had been talking to the stranger in the school after church; the fellow said he was from the War Department. That was that, but the rumour is going round now that he was doing a tour of the islands trying to get some of the landlords and people like that to form a part-time regiment of soldiers. Big Neil doesn't like the idea at all!'

'I know; I heard my father and him talking about it. My father thinks Hitler's making fools of us, and that we should stand up to him right now.'

'Let's hope they're wrong. Big Neil has seen two wars already and your father has seen one – and that's enough for both of them. I suppose I've been one of the lucky ones. Nobody ever thought it worthwhile to call me up, and if they didn't think it last time they certainly won't think it now. Mind you, I'm the kind they should take – the kind that's no good for anything else!'

I thought he was going to embark on one of his self-pitying monologues. But no. Old Hector, whose opinion few people ever sought and who was normally too retiring to volunteer it, was clearly an avid reader of the newspapers although he made great play of his own lack of education. For the next half hour I was treated to a simple lecture on the rise of Nazi Germany, and it was only the descent of the dark that finally brought me to my feet. On my way out I noticed his navy blue serge jacket draped over the back of a chair.

'Why have you got your Sunday suit hanging out? Are you going somewhere?' I was only pulling his leg, because Hector had never been known to leave the village since he stopped ghillying. I noticed but didn't really register that what I could see of his face in the dark looked vaguely shifty for a moment. 'Oh, that,' he said. And then, quickly recovering his old easy manner, 'Are you forgetting the Moderator's visit? With one thing and another I haven't had time to put it back in the trunk.' I left him and went racing down the hill, suddenly filled with excitement at the prospect of a war on the horizon. None of the implications of it worried my young mind of course but, suddenly, the idea seemed rather splendid. The wars of my schoolbooks were wars of heroics and romance and totally unreal; my father's war was shrouded in silence and as unreal as the rest. But the prospect of a war on my own doorstep and in my own time was exhilarating, and I found myself wishing that I were older – ready to don a khaki uniform with brass buttons on the shoulders, or a navy blue one with gold plastered on the cap; the airforce didn't have a very glamorous tradition as yet, but I remembered what my father had said the day the first aeroplane landed on the sands, the day Maggie MacGeachan had been buried. 'These are the things of the new wars,' he had said. 'These are the things with the power of good and evil; they'll be lifting people to the beach down there to the hospital when there's an emergency like a burst appendix or something, and somewhere else they'll be dropping death on people from the skies.'

'Is there going to be a war?' I asked him when I got home.

'Probably,' he said. 'And the sooner the better!'

'John!' There was no mistaking the horror in my mother's face.

'It's true,' he said. 'Every extra day we give that madman the more powerful he'll become; and this damn government we've got thinks it'll buy him off with sweet and reasonable arguments. We're always the same, hoping things will work out. We're too used to winning, that's our trouble; this time we might be in for a big surprise.'

'You're not saying we'll lose!' My chauvinism was well founded in the glories of the Empire.

'No, because we've also got a habit of winning. But it's not going to be as easy as some people think. Some fool in the newspaper was talking of the united world crushing Hitler in a few weeks if war breaks out. Some hopes. For a start the Yanks

100

will come in and pick up the medals when somebody else has done the dirty work. Anyway, who wants to talk of war? You've got a whole new world opening up for you in a week's time. Tarbert may be only a tuppeny-ha'penny village as far as the rest of the world is concerned, but for you it's the golden gates.'

He went back to repairing a boot which he had wedged on to a three-headed last; he had finished pinning on a new leather sole and now he was trimming it with a knife and a rasp. I knew that he wouldn't hear anything else even if I tried to pursue the conversation; when he did start on a job his concentration was total. My brother hadn't even looked up when I came in; he was equally deeply involved in a jig-saw puzzle that some visiting relative had given him and, in any case, as the time for my departure drew nearer the same gulf seemed to be developing between him and me as between me and Gillespie, who had opted not to continue with school after fourteen. Over on St Clement's bench my mother was putting the last stitches into a jacket which had been handed down to me from my young banker cousin, and apart from that one word of remonstration to my father she had remained engrossed in her own task – but, I could sense from the automatic rhythm of her stitching, lost in a private world of her own too. We had recently acquired a double wick oil-lamp of the kind that clipped on to the wall and from its height it cast a semi-circular pool of light which spread out to take in the three of them as they bent over their different tasks. Where I sat, just inside the door, the edge of the light had begun to diffuse with the darkness and I found myself feeling like a stranger looking in on a world of other people, and I suddenly felt lonely at the thought of the golden gates.

Next morning I was winding my way as usual to milk Primrose, revived by a night's sleep and the thought that this was one chore that I would be leaving behind me. I was trudging along with my eyes on my toes and so I was almost beside him when I noticed Old Hector standing at the roadside, obviously waiting for the morning bus that travelled northwards to Tarbert and on to Stornoway in Lewis. I suddenly realised that he'd been lying to me (or at least being devious) about the Sunday suit the night before. Because now he was wearing it – dressed to the nines in fact, in a white celluloid collar and tie, a crotal and white Harris Tweed cap, and a polished pair of delicate shoes that he probably hadn't worn since Singapore. He was leaning on a hefty walking stick, puffing at his pipe and staring into the distance like a man with doom on his mind.

'Wh – where are you going?' I asked.

'On the bus,' he said sarcastically without removing his pipe. 'I've reached an age when I'm allowed out on my own.' I felt myself flushing at the snub, but I decided to make no retort and moved up the hill to find Primrose.

'Where was Old Hector going?' everybody I met that day asked me, and I seemed to meet half the village. 'He hasn't left the village in years. Where was he going?'

'Woolworth's,' I replied, not liking to admit that he hadn't let me into his confidence.

'Woolworth's! What the devil can he want in Woolworth's that Jackie the driver couldn't bring him, or the tweed landry?' The Harris Tweed trade had begun to boom to such an extent that a regular lorry now came round from a Stornoway textile mill to supply the weavers with yarn for contracted-out tweeds, and it, of course, was contributing its share to the well-being of the villages as an unofficial public service vehicle. 'Woolworth's!' said somebody else. 'It's well seen his sister Maggie isn't alive or he wouldn't be going off gallivanting and spending money in Woolworth's.'

If Maggie was alive he wouldn't be needing to go on the bus, I thought to myself as I made my way through a long and guilty day.

The return bus from Stornoway wasn't due back till long after the evening milking, so after I'd seen to Primrose I decided to stay on in Hector's house and keep the fire in for his return and have the kettle boiling. The first warning I had of his arrival was the thud of his walking-stick as he flung it into a corner, and the softer flump of his cap as he threw it on to the wooden seat below the window.

'How did it go?' I asked, thankful that the walking-stick was out of his hand.

'Go?' he said. 'Go!' He obviously didn't remember that I didn't know officially where he was; he was also confirming that he had been exactly where I thought he had been. But it was a relief to know that his anger wasn't directed at me for once; in fact he was almost appealing to me to join in his wrath.

'I've never been so insulted in my life! She was sixty if she was a day and, judging by the streaky red hair of her, there was tinker blood in her. For sure there was plenty tinker in her talk. And if God ever gave a man a warning it was there in the shape of her mother who will never see ninety-eight again – all fankled up with arthritis except for her tongue ... and she had the nerve to make remarks about my legs!'

'So you're not taking the daughter?' I ventured.

'Take her!' he spluttered. 'It was a job lot man. Whoever is fool enough to take that one has to take the mother as well. It wasn't a man she was wanting, it was a caretaker! We didn't say in our advertisement that we wanted a woman who would come and live here; she was all set to have me move in there. Me live in Lewis! I'd be a laughing-stock for the few days that I survived ...'

He said a lot more than that, but I had relaxed once I'd heard him refer to the advert as 'our advertisement'. I was relieved to know that he wasn't holding me personally responsible for the day, and, after that all I had to do was to keep a straight face till he got the anger out of his system.

'Would you like a cup of tea?' I asked. 'The kettle's boiling.'

'Ach you're a good lad. See, Jackie the driver offered me a cigarette and I took it and slipped it into my pocket for you.' For a moment I could have sworn that I caught a whiff of whisky as he patted me on the shoulder and sat down in his own chair for the first time since he came in. 'Aye,' he said. 'A cup of tea would be just fine; it's more than I was offered in that place.'

I should have left things at that, I suppose, but some devil must have prompted me.

'And when are you going to see the next one?' I asked – unfortunately just as he took a large mouthful of tea. I thought I was going to have to thump him on the back to get him breathing again. But he recovered.

'The next one!' he gasped. 'You must be out of your mind or you must think I'm out of mine. There's going to be no next one! I'd rather sell Primrose and make do with nessels for the rest of my life.'

'Are you forgetting breach of promise? And the price of Primrose won't be the half of what you'll have to pay.'

'What the devil have you done to me?' gasped Hector, putting his teacup on the floor and his head in his hands. I slipped off home without replying.

'Woolworth's must have put a spell on Hector MacGeachan,' somebody said to me a few days later. The atmosphere between us had been distinctly chilly for the last few days and it was only on the evening before his second safari that he had told me, almost casually, that he was setting off on his travels again. He encouraged no discussion. On the evening of his second journey I took care to have the milking finished and be clear of his house before the night bus came back from Stornoway, and next morning it was with a certain amount of trepidation that I wound my way up the hill. To my astonishment he was waiting for me in great good form with a letter in his hand. But neither then nor ever after did he refer to his trip, and it will become easy to see why I couldn't possibly raise the subject.

'Here, I want you to post this letter for me. Here's a penny ha'penny to buy a stamp, and I want you to put the letter in the pillar-box yourself and *not* hand it to Calum the Post. I'm writing as you can see to that woman on the island, and if she'll have me I'm taking her, as they say, "unseen".'

'You can't do that!'

'Stop telling me what I can and can't do,' he growled. 'I survived all these years with my sister Maggie, so I reckon that I can cope with most things now. I'm going off for a sack of peat. You get on with the milking of Primrose. And don't mention that letter to a living soul.'

The inter-islands post was uncertain and slow in those days, and I knew that Hector couldn't possibly get a reply before I left for High School.

'What'll happen to Old Hector and Primrose?' I asked my mother as she packed my case the night before the day. 'You won't be able to milk her night and morning, day in day out.'

'Don't you worry about Old Hector; I've been talking to the women and we'll take it in turns to milk the cow for him till he gets her sold at the October sales. And after that we'll see to it that he's all right for milk; despite what your father says I don't see Hector adapting to nessels at his age.'

I smiled to myself. I had an idea that Hector was going to have to adapt to rather more than condensed milk in the next month or two.

Chapter Eight

Every year since school began I had gone to the Northlands to Big Grandfather's for the whole duration of the summer holiday and in recent years, since a regular bus service had been established, I had travelled each way alone. This time my father was going to accompany me; it was as if I was being ceremonially handed over into fosterage. I suppose that's how it must have felt to my parents too. High School was only sixteen miles away and today, if the circumstances were the same, I would be expected to commute – travelling twenty minutes each way by school bus. But times were different; the state of the road was vastly different; buses were different and their regularity uncertain. Therefore, from now on, I would be coming home only for the statutory school holidays and for occasional long week-ends. From that August day onward it would be from the outside that I would see the village ageing – the village which I love more than any place on earth. And that is how it has been. It has always been as a visitor that I have returned ... and, increasingly, as a stranger.

My parents must have realised that. They must have known that only failure (in terms of the island philosophy of the time) would bring me back to a life in the village. I had 'done my homework' ... I had learnt 'to talk English' ... I had 'won the bursary' ... I had done all the things that would launch me for far shores. And I was as excited as any man setting off on a voyage – too young to care that I was leaving the people who had moulded my life … my parents themselves, Great Aunt Rachel, the Boer War veteran, the man with the hole in his cheek, Old Hector and all the others whom I know now to have shaped my character and my attitudes. Others would wield their different influences in times to come, but they would be only adding daubs and touches of better and worse. It was the knowledge of the beginning of finality that made my mother give me a hasty peck on the cheek, and made my father sound brusque as he picked up my case and said 'Here comes the bus; come along!' We walked down to the gate dressed as if we were setting off to some formal function. He had his good plus-four suit on; I was in my first pair of long trousers which made me feel as if I was walking with my knees in splints.

The bus was long for the roads and Jackie was out to impress a larger complement of passengers than usual. Every time we hit a pot-hole – and there were plenty of them – we were detonated six inches off our seats to come back down with a thud; here and there a man muttered an expletive and a couple of holy women groaned. Jackie was trying to make up time, waging a losing battle with the unpunctuality which his employers were trying to iron out of him, knowing that his stops would be more frequent than usual because of the 'scholars' going back to school. Four times he stopped before leaving the village behind him, each time to pick up a well-dressed boy or girl with a suitcase; they were the ones who had gone the bursary road before me.

I was setting out on the journey to my future and yet, in a sense, it was a journey back in time. A century before, helpless and hopeless bands of people must have plodded northwards on a track along that same route; they were the displaced persons of their time, callously thrown off the lush agricultural ground of the Southlands by overlords who decided to follow the profitable fashion of the mainland and turn their estates into sheepfarms. Sheepfarming didn't require large numbers of workers; on the contrary tenants were taking up valuable land that could be put under sheep, and so the people were shunted out of their homelands and crowded into the dour rocky north. Generations later I was born in those Northlands just as the trend was at last being reversed, and as a child I had travelled south with my parents as they set out to reclaim the

106

old lands and build a new village. A decade had now passed since we jolted in a decrepit bus on our journey to our promised land. The Atlantic had been on our right then and we had threaded our way through empty country – a country which became greener and more inviting the farther south we went. Now, those ten years later, the sea was on the left and I was travelling the route northwards – through new villages that had sprouted along the shore in quick succession after the apparently successful establishment of our own. Only their names were old – memorials to the ancient Viking exploration of those lands. Horgabost, Crago, Seileabost, and finally Luskentyre strung out along one of the most spectacular beaches in Britain. These were the villages of the people who had returned to reclaim the good land for themselves and they were now out to prove that they could coax prosperity from it. Time would tell.

After the Luskentyre road-end the landscape changed as the bland machair lands of the south gave way to the dour Northlands with acres of grey rock resisting the tough stunted heather which didn't have enough soil beneath it to allow it to grow into cover. Here and there miniscular peatbanks had been discovered by the men of the north who would labour to pick out seams that would each surrender only a couple of creels of winter fuel. It was a landscape I had passed through many times without noticing it, but now I was seeing it with fresh eyes and comparing those scars of peat with the long trenches on our own moorlands. Here and there hessian sacks of peat were stacked by the roadside waiting to be transported by lorry to Tarbert; now and again a man and wife would wave to the bus before bending back to the business of filling more sacks to add to their pile.

Just before the wicked crook of road known as The Devil's Elbow the bus crested the high hill and the view burst open on to the bays of Miavag and Kendebig and, further on, the mouth of East Loch Tarbert with the island of Scalpay sitting squat bastion against the Minch. I was looking down on peopled territory once again and I could see the chequered pattern those people had dug out of the heather with spade and pick to give themselves tillable patches around their homes. And for all the poverty of the land there was an air of gentle prosperity; well-established white houses had steadily displaced most of the thatched houses. They owed nothing to the land, those houses; they had been built with money from fishing or, most usually, with money sent home by sailor sons, and daughters in service in the mansions of the mainland cities. It was no shame to be in service. Far from it. Those girls, like their sailor brothers, were repaying their debt to ageing parents to whom some would, themselves, return one day with some of the city's sophistication showing in their manners and their clothes and their luggage. They wouldn't all come back, of course. Many of the girls, in particular, would marry city husbands and swell the Highland coteries of Glasgow and Edinburgh and London: each one who did return would marry, not too late in life, a man from home and rear a family into which she would instill a longing for the bright lights.

As the bus moved carefully down the Heel of Kendebig its progress became easier and conversation was allowed to develop, not only because the bumping stopped, but because passengers who have no private sorrows always become more voluble with relief at the approach of the journey's end. The reason for the greater comfort was that we were now on the new tarmacadam surface which was gently snaking its way out south from Tarbert where it had begun in the time honoured tradition that improvement always begins at the centre of local government and at the doorsteps of its representatives. The marvel of the 'tar road' was a subject for conversation in itself; it was a miracle of our time although it had taken six score years to reach us.

On the right we passed Wee Grandfather's house from where my family had set out on our odyssey ten years ago; my father looked into the middle distance and bit on his pipe but I would never know whether he wondered if his move had been a wise one. I knew that my mother had never got over her longing for the Northlands, but I never knew with him.

On the left was the flat no man's land where the tinkers camped in summer; I felt my face flushing as I remembered my encounter with the crude siren of their tribe. In the moonlight the coppery red of her hair and her silhouette had convinced me that she must be the glamorous accommodating maid from the doctor's house. Accommodating she had proved to be but, alas, more willing than I was able and I had been unable to verify whether the Johnsonian dictum regarding the chambermaid and the Duchess applied to the tinker girl and the doctor's maid. I was mightily relieved to see that the gipsy encampment had been uplifted for the winter. Would she recognise me again, I wondered? And hoped not.

My father drew my attention to the water-driven wool mill which two enterprising brothers had opened in neat time for the latest boom in Harris Tweed; there the crofters sent the raw fleeces to be combed and carded and sent back as long thin sausages of soft wool for hand-spinning; the very boom that had made them was on the point of breaking them because the demand for tweed now far exceeded what the hand-spinners could satisfy and, more and more, the mills of Stornoway were turning out ready-spun thread and the spinning wheels would soon be making their ways to the antique shops of the cities. 'That's progress for you,' my father said. 'Soon they'll be making Harris Tweed in Japan and that'll be that.' As he finished speaking he put his pipe in his pocket and put his cap on. We were approaching the red gate which my grandfather felt obliged to keep painted red since it had become a landmark, and I could see the old man standing waiting for us.

The uneasy relationship which I remembered from boyhood had disappeared from between my father and the old man, and a vague mutual respect had taken its place; it never flourished into friendship because Big Grandfather had never, I think, fully accepted that the match had ever been worthy of my mother. Grandfather was a pragmatist who had built around himself a solid core of respectability; he had moved his family from black house to white; he had saved enough money from his days at sea to be able to surround himself with the trappings of modest comfort; he had built up a sheepstock against the odds in a barren land, and he had become an expert on sheep-rearing; he had seen his elder daughter through school and college into the teaching profession in days when education had not yet achieved predominant importance; he had seen a strong, intelligent son develop into a master craftsman as a cabinet-maker. Backed up by Wee Grannie whose roly-poly appearance belied a very sharp, shrewd brain he had built up a pillarship of community from which my mother had been plucked by a man of books and dreams. In the early days Big Grandfather had courteously upbraided and cajoled, and my father had smiled and remained unruffled. Now each accepted the other for the quality of total honesty that they had in common.

'Well, I've brought him to you,' my father said. 'He's been warned to do what he's told and to be a help to you around the place.'

'He's never been any trouble here,' said my grandfather, leading the way down the winding path to the house by the shore. 'He's never been any trouble to his grandmother or myself.' I was glad that the old man seemed to have forgotten my visit of the previous summer when I had put the effervescent salts into the pee-pot below the bed being occupied by two holy lady visitors and caused them to flood or, rather, froth the house! Grandfather had confined me to barracks for a week then, vowing that the shame of my behaviour would haunt him forever. The shame had obviously been exorcised. 'So long as he's home before dark and keeps away from the craobhag … that's all I'll expect from him. And that he brings home a trout from the burn now and again.'

'And gets stuck into his books,' said my father pointedly.

'Hum!' said the old man, and changed the conversation to talk of the weather and the sheep-stock, to which my father responded with as much enthusiasm as he could muster. I knew that he would stay for a meal and then make his way back to his own parents' house where he would spend the night before catching the morning bus back to the Southlands; there was a finality about the prospect which gave me slight stirrings of apprehension; but they disappeared as the smell of Wee Grannie's cooking wafted to meet us while we were still a hundred yards from the house.

'We'll just take your case straight up the stairs and your grandmother will show you where to put your things later on.'

My father went into the living room and I could hear Wee Grannie and himself exchanging pleasantries as I followed grandfather upstairs. Over the years, under the guidance of my uncle who was now away in Southampton, he'd had the house modernised. In addition to the very comfortable living room downstairs there was also a drawing-room-cum-dining-room

110

'for best' furnished with a magnificent red mahogany expanding table which could pull out to seat twelve on occasions like the twice yearly communions, twelve mahogany chairs covered in horse-hair that used to prickle the backs of my knees but wouldn't any more now that I was in long trousers for good, and a large elegant side-board with a tall mirror; in addition, it had two comfortable armchairs on each side of a maroon-tiled fireplace flanked by two spotted china dogs and brass fire-irons. Heavy Victorian velvet curtains gave it a slightly gloomy air in summer but made it cosy in winter, and they trapped the heady smell of the geraniums which my grandmother nurtured carefully from year to year.

The stairs in themselves were a fascination for me – brought up in the over-crowded little corrugated-iron two-roomed house in the Southlands; they led up to two large bedrooms which had recently been made even more spacious by having had dormer windows added to them; in their own room my grandparents had decided to retain the closed in box-beds, but the spare room had been refurbished in a crisp modern style and had a musty camphory smell except when it was aired for visitors. My room was the small coomb-ceilinged one between the other two; it had a bed with brass knobs on it, and I would have it all to myself; on the opposite wall from it was a bookcase fashioned out of two orange-boxes with white lace draped over them, with a brass oil-lamp sitting on top; the chest-of-drawers for my clothes was placed with a mirror on it right under a sky-light which, when it was propped open, let in the smell of the shore, the call of the seabirds and the morning and evening chugging of the fishing boats coming in to Tarbert pier. As grandfather threw open the door I could see that the whole room had been papered and painted afresh against my arrival, and a neat little woollen rug had been placed in front of the bed to protect my feet from the cold of the linoleum. I stopped and stared. This was to be my room – my very own, private room – for three years, and the thrill of its comfort and its privacy was something I have never captured since even in the plushest hotel.

'What's that?' I asked, pointing to a small pile of clothes and a leather harness-type satchel on the quilt.

'O, your Great-Aunt Christina brought these for you; the

111

twins had them when they were in school.' The twins were two manly second cousins of mine (one of them was now the banker who had prompted my reply to the doctor); they were quite a few years older than I was and it might take me a little time to grow into their well-kept school clothes, but the satchel was something which would come in useful right away. I fingered it, trying to look casual, but deep down I was thrilled; up till then I had always carried my books to school in a bundle tied with string – tucking them under my jersey to keep them dry when it rained. The satchel was yet another symbol of the new age!

'Right, we'd better go back downstairs or you'll be getting a sharp touch of your grannie's tongue before you're an hour in the house if you're not ready to sit at the table when she lifts the meal. And there's something I want to show you privately.'

He led me downstairs but instead of turning into the living room where I could hear my father and grandmother in animated conversation about Harris Tweed he turned right and opened the door into a closet which had always been a junk room – although as with everything else in grandfather's house, tidily ordered – the room in which I had occasionally been made to camp when the house was full of communion or cattle-sale visitors. I couldn't imagine what there could be to see in the closet. But when Big Grandfather opened the door, it was a junk room no longer. Instead it had a wash basin with two taps, a flush toilet and a full length bath. I'd had no idea that the old man had had 'the water brought in' as it was popularly known, and this was a totally new dimension to my world – a slightly embarrassing one. Although some of the new white houses in our own village had had interior plumbing installed, we hadn't, and I'd never had occasion to experiment with bath or toilet. Taps, yes. When our school had been modernised the outhouses had been fitted with chemical toilets but nobody had ever used them, and the brass taps in the cloakrooms gushed only cold water. In neighbours' houses a visitor would never have dreamt of making indelicate use of the facilities and one didn't go visiting in order to wash one's hands. While I was admiring the black and white tiled linoleum and marvelling at the clinical appearance of it all, grandfather was turning the taps on and off and talking about a bath every Saturday night.

'And now look here,' he said. 'This is something your grannie can't very well explain to you. We've got no river on this croft as you have at home so that water from a well up at the back has to be stored in a big concrete tank that you'll see out there on the hillock behind the house. The tank takes a long time to fill up so we have to conserve the water as much as possible. You'll still be pee-ing outside, of course, unless you're caught short at night but don't pull the plug after a pee. You do your shitties in here, and you use that paper there afterwards; that's when you must be sure to press this lever here.' And he demonstrated by flushing the toilet. I seemed to be entering into several new worlds all at once.

My father stopped to relieve himself at the end of the byre as he set off to his own parents' house after the meal. 'Did you see the new bathroom?' I asked him.

'Aye,' he said. 'You'll be taking unkindly to using the outside when you come home at Christmas. That's progress for you. There was an old man in Lewis whose son married a stylish girl from the mainland and she insisted on turning one of the rooms of the house into a bathroom. Very stylish she was and not at all used to the ways of Lewis. One thing she couldn't stand was the smell of salt herring boiling and didn't she insist that if the old man wanted to continue eating potatoes and salt herring he had to eat them outside. One of the neighbours couldn't believe it one day when he came along and found the old fellow outside at the end of the house with a big platter of potatoes and salt herring on his knee. *What the devil are you doing eating outside?* the neighbour asked. *It's the way of the new world, man,* the old fellow replied. *There was a time when I ate inside and shat outside, but now I shit inside and eat out!'*

'That's not true,' I laughed.

'Maybe not,' he said. 'But there's truth in it. A lot of your world is going to be turned upside down and inside out from tomorrow; and most of it will be for the best. Ach well –' He dug into his pocket. 'I know your mother has given you a bit of money for your pocket and she'll be sending you some in the post from time to time. Here's half-a-crown for extra.' He paused and his eyes crinkled in a way that he had. 'Well, so long my boy – and good luck'. He shook hands with me for the first time in his life, and walked briskly away without looking back. I stood looking after him till the dusk closed round him at

113

the red gate. I was alone on the pathway in the gloom; the house was out of sight round an elbow of the path. A few lights twinkled far away across the bay on the island of Scalpay, accentuating the utter solitude. I felt the chill of the evening and a prickling at the back of my eyes, and I could almost see in my mind's eye my mother and my three brothers in the hot little living room back in the village.

A little tin oil-lamp, hanging on the wall, lit up the stair down which my grandmother was making her slow progress as I got in. She was breathing heavily and carefully putting the same foot in front of her on each new tread as she came down, and, for the first time, I realised that she was getting very old.

'I've been putting a hot bottle in your bed just for tonight,' she said. 'And I've laid out your clothes for school tomorrow. There's a glass of milk and some oatcakes on the table, and your grandfather's waiting to take the book when you're finished.' The usual phrase for morning and evening prayers was 'taking the books' but Wee Grandmother, for some reason that I've never fathomed, spoke her native Gaelic with immaculate purity and rhythm but with occasional archaisms and highly individual usages. The bible was 'the book' one and indivisible stretching from the Genesis to her present moment of time. Grandfather treated God with immaculate courtesy but was precise as to the time set aside for Him. He conducted morning worship at quarter past eight (at home we hadn't ever held morning prayers) and at night he invariably reached for the bible and his gold rimmed spectacles at half past ten. He had his own tall mahogany chair with slim arms on it on one side of the fire; Grannie had a Taransay chair with a plaited straw seat on the other; I sat on the newly acquired modern couch which they both called a 'dive in'. Prayers that night were as they would be every night for three years. Grandfather prayed, sitting in his chair; he then read a psalm and a chapter which he always seemed to know almost word perfectly, but if he faltered Grannie would prompt him from her memory; when he was finished he gave exactly the same kind of sigh every night and we all got down on our knees while he prayed – first to a set formula and then, discursively, taking in events of topical concern. When he was finished he straightened up and yawned and said 'Well, woman ...' and waited for her to

114

precede him upstairs after he had seen to his dogs in the scullery. 'You'll blow your own lamp out,' he said as he left the room. 'Don't fall asleep with it on or you'll smoke us all out.' I couldn't believe my ears. Father had a well-founded holy terror of fire and would never have dreamt of letting anybody put out the last flame of the evening without checking it himself. This was another freedom that I was going to enjoy.

I was wakened in the morning by the chugging of the fishing boats and the screeching of their escorts of gulls. I had no idea what the time was so I opened the skylight and just stood in my shirt tails staring out at a scene that couldn't possibly be more different from the one I was accustomed to at home. It wasn't a totally new scene to me; I had seen it at holiday times over the years but now I felt it, strangely, part of my life, whereas then I'd been a visitor and an onlooker. There were, I suppose, half a dozen boats in the bay with their Kelvin paraffin engines hammering out their staccatos, and through the alternating fury and exultation of the seagulls I could hear the men shouting to each other from boat to boat as they folded their nets and flung unwanted squid and shrimp and crab overboard to the frenzied birds; the morning was so still that I could hear their conversations as they compared news of their catches and bits of gossip. Occasionally they would break into English which, even to me, was painfully ungrammatical, as they included a boat which had an east coast number on her shoulder. I had completely forgotten the purpose of my morning till I heard Big Grandfather shouting from the foot of the stairs, demanding to know if I was deliberately trying to be late for my first morning of High School.

'You know where the school is?' he enquired as he spooned his brose.

'Man, your memory worries me,' Grannie said. 'Don't you remember the boy went to the infant school here for a while when the family had the measles that year?'

I had almost forgotten myself; or, rather, I hadn't associated that Primary School with the one I was going to join now. 'Yes, of course,' I said. 'Instead of turning right down through the town at the foot of Caw Brae I go straight on past the Doctor's manse to the east side.'

'It'll take you fifteen minutes if you run part of the way,' grandfather went on. 'And that means that you'll have to move smartly at the dinner hour if you're going to have time for a decent dinner –'

'Which you're going to have,' Grannie cut in firmly. 'You're not going to be spending money in Tommy's on rubbish at eleven o'clock and then coming home here without an appetite for your food!'

Tommy's shop! I'd forgotten that a shrewd distant relative of our own had opened up a little grocery store just across the road from the school, and it had developed into a tuck shop to which the Headmaster tended to turn a blind eye even though there was a strict school law that no pupils were to leave the school playground except at the lunch hour and at four o'clock. Few rules were honoured more in the breech ... and I made a mental note to pop upstairs for some pennies before setting off. I thought Big Grandfather's morning prayers would never end but, at last, I found myself with my empty satchel on my back trotting up to the red gate and the main road. A small number of youngsters, all with the crispness of first day of term about them, were walking along the road in their ones and twos; they had a casual air about them that suggested that the journey was not a new one for them. But they were all strangers to me and I jogged on alone.

The best view of the town of Tarbert (for town it is called despite the fact that it's a village by mainland standards) is the view that was discovered by the first of the picture-postcard photographers many years ago. And it will never be improved on – from land, sea or air. It is the view as one stands at the top of the steep hill known as the Caw and leans over the stone dyke that protects one from the sheer drop down to the near shore of the bay. From there the town is seen in the entirety of it that matters – from the hotel on the far left the eye is drawn along the shore road known as 'the street' which edges the far side of the harbour and leads down to the pier. It isn't a crescent quite, but near enough. It is, despite what many people tend to think, the new town – the town that grew up when the mailboat began to ply across the Minch connecting Tarbert to the mainland, thereby making it the principal centre of commerce from which it grew into a capital. Tarbert is the Gaelic for isthmus and only a scrawny neck of land separates east loch from west. In the old days of Clan MacLeod and the big estate owners who bought them out, sea traffic had been down the west coast, down from Huisinis and Amhuinnsuidhe of the great castle, down by the off-shore islands of Scarp and Taransay and all the way to the rich green machair lands where the new villages of my own boyhood are now ageing. But with the opening of the steamer route and the building of the road all that had changed; West Tarbert had become a mini-suburbia and East Tarbert had begun to bustle.

There were fourteen shops in the year that I went to High School, for the town now served the whole hinterland with its scrabble of villages. As I paused at the top of Caw I could see the whole sweep of the town and from my memory of summer holidays I could identify all the shops. Nine of them were general stores – different from each other only according to the characters that their owners had stamped on them; in most of them you could buy anything from a foot of black-twist pipe tobacco to a tether for a cow or a bag of nails and a hammer. Five were special – the baker, the cobbler, the butcher, the watchmaker, and 'the black man's' – owned by Ali Mohammed, who was now an established member of the community and was called Alick. And there were the institutions – the large ones like the big white Bank of Scotland with the manager's house on top of it, the pier office, the Church of Scotland and the Free Presbyterian Church, each with its own manse. There were discreet offices too, like the one where a registrar lurked who put births and marriages and deaths on files; there were offices which were beginning to classify people into sick and deserving poor and the rest. People lived there too, above and beside their places of business. All the buildings, in a higgledy-piggledy of styles, hugged the one side of the street like a row of pensioners holding hands, and, alone on the nearside to me stood the tall war memorial with red fuchsia growing up round a lot of names.

The street still seemed asleep as I watched it, with the shop doors still closed. But smoke was beginning to rise and, here and there, a house door opened and someone with a satchel would slip out. Like the country road along which I'd come the street was beginning to move with the ones and twos heading for the school and I moved down the Caw to join the stream at

117

the junction of the road and the street where the country met the town. Three boys were coming along together, chatting earnestly like old friends. One was lean and sophisticated with the air of someone who'd been around for a while and knew the ropes; one was large with an unruly mane and a white laugh; one was sturdy and serious looking, with a suggestion of a seaman's walk. They had the assurance of each other's company; I was the country mouse come to town. The older boy spoke to me and asked my name and where I came from, and I told him. It turned out that he was, indeed, in his final year and that his two companions were rookies like myself. They were to be my companions through the High School and beyond, till the time came about which people were then only beginning to worry.

Chapter Nine

There were more pupils assembled in the grounds of the High School on that morning in late August than the total of those who had passed through the doors of the old school that I had left in the Southlands in the forty-five years of its existence. Tarbert School was two schools in one: one section of it was the Primary School for the town and its hinterland, and the other the High School to which pupils graduated in their early teens from more than a score of village schools throughout the whole of Harris. It had a grand name, after a landlord who had been its benefactor at the end of last century, and the technical description of it was Junior Secondary School. But it was known as Tarbert School, and that was that.

Awe is the second-last thing to which a lump of a boy will admit, but if it wasn't with awe it was certainly with a great amount of wonderment and a flittering of trepidation, that I stared round the motley throng as I clung close to my new-found companions. The threads of the Hebridean tapestry were all there – the fair hair and the blue eyes of the Norse incomers of nine centuries ago, the brown-eyed Iberian strain which was my own, and the jet black hair and the blue eyes of the Celt. But it wasn't heredity or pedigree that occupied my mind, but the thought that any moment now I would be coming face to face with the Headmaster whose legend was monster for discipline – the man who had moulded the whole character of the school and given it a formidable reputation for learning although his own education was home-spun to the extent of his never having attended college or University. He had carved his way up from being a pupil-teacher in his youth, achieving the status of teacher through an informal apprenticeship long before the various education laws demanded diplomas or degrees. He had a reputation for choleric temper and ferocious Presbyterianism – a combination more explosive than Nobel's imaginings. I had never heard him referred to by his proper name; to the whole community (behind his back, of course) he was 'The Blus' because of his eccentric pronunciation of the arithmetical additional symbol; his character would never have permitted of him being called 'The Minors' although he had that one wrong too. I didn't have long to wait to meet him. An imperious whistle sounded, and when I turned round there he was at the top of the school steps – a sturdy figure in a well cut plus-four suit of much finer tweed than our Harris variety; he had a shock of greying hair, a strong face which looked as if it could hide a smile deep down for a special occasion, and shrewd hazel eyes behind gold-rimmed spectacles. As soon as the whistle sounded a silence fell over the playground and, herded by the veterans, we scuffed our ways into our respective male and female lines. As we filed in he stood like a traffic policeman directing us. Third year to the science room. Second year to the English room. First year to his own room. It didn't require much education to know that the last category was my own.

Angus Macdonald (for that was his real name) was the only example of the archetypal dominie that I ever came across; he was probably a member of the last generation of the species. His own subjects were Latin and Gaelic and he taught them both with a ferocity which he reinforced, as he did discipline, with a supple leather Lochgelly tawse. But he didn't ply it with the sadism in which that first teacher of my childhood had revelled; he used it as the third arm of authority. In my three years under his tutelage I heard him miscalled and cursed with adolescent enthusiasm but I never once heard him accused of unfairness. Every single line of the Goldsmith evocation applied to him; not least that

> ... he was kind; or if severe in aught
> The love he bore to learning was in fault.

Not the least of his influences on me was that he taught me, for the first time, that my own native language was a language of aged culture and literature and not a crude dialect to be scourged out of my consciousness as an aberration of heritage or as something 'of no commercial value, and a barrier to advancement in the world'.

'The Blus' (his name was never used without the definite article) was backed by two young men of totally different attitudes to teaching. They were in their twenties – youthful and enthusiastic – and they regarded their students as young adults with whom they could joke and laugh and for whom they could bring their respective class-room subjects to life. Their relationships with us were much more that of tutors than teachers. Over the years Alexander Nicholson was to build on the love of English and history which my primary teacher and my father had nurtured in me; Leslie Watson came to accept with unswerving good grace that the most he could ever hope to teach me from the rich realms of mathematics and science was that Pythagoras was the one who adorned triangles with squares and that Archimedes was the one who had the bath. What those two young men did find in me – which neither I nor anybody else had ever suspected – was that I had a sense of humour and, by encouraging it, they helped me grow out of the 'please miss, yes miss' attitudes of infant school and discover that learning was a process of doubting and questioning in which there could be fun.

It took remarkably little time to adjust to the size of the new school after the cosy menage of thirteen in which I had spent most of my school life hitherto. The most difficult thing to get used to was the formality of a large class in which everybody concentrated on the same subject instead of eight little units at different stages and involved in different themes. Gone was the hum of activity and the pervasive smell of chalk; in their place was an almost tangible feel of concentration. Gone too was the innocent informality of little boys and girls sharing desks; now the boys were grouped on one side of the room and on the other was a uniformity of gym-slips belted to suggest varying promises of chests.

Within a week or two I was marching from classroom to classroom at change-over time as if I had stridden those

121

corridors all my life. The awe of the second and third year boys vanished as I packed into the urinal with them at the intervals to snatch quick smokes while somebody kept cave at the door. Occasionally The Blus would take it into his head to do a tour of the premises, but the most brazen of us merely cupped our cigarettes in our hands and pulled them up into our sleeves, swinging our arms to dispel the smoke while his head was thrust into the reeking hazy atmosphere demanding to know what we were doing 'crowded in here on a lovely day like this' as if he feared we might be getting up to some of the more unorthodox sophistications of the great Public Schools. One soon learnt that The Blus, for all this thundering, didn't really expect boys to behave themselves – he had seen too many boys for that – but he did expect them not to get caught. His rule and his role were equally extraordinary.

Most of the country pupils were in formal lodgings with landladies who meticulously took their money every Friday; a few like myself, for reasons of kinship and poverty, were guests with relatives who deemed it more blest to give than to receive. The lodgers set the pattern of life. They had to be back in their digs each evening at six o'clock for their meals and their landladies, who took their responsibilities seriously and were frequently in cahoots with the headmaster, expected their charges to remain indoors for the rest of the evening and do their homework unless there was an organised fishing trip or a rare social function. Between the hours of four and six the boys and girls were free to do as they chose although, in all conscience, there was little to do except parade up and down the street, look into the shop windows, or hang over the sea-wall watching the occasional fishing boat coming in with its covey of quarrelling gulls. Now and then a boat with unfamiliar registration lettering would attract us down to the pier itself and we would listen uncomprehendingly to the east coast chatter of men from faraway places like Peterhead or Stonehaven or Buckie as they spoke in a language that was almost English but not quite. On two evenings a week the mailboat *Lochmor* would shoulder her way in from the Minch and for an hour or so the village would be en fête as the bulk of the population congregated on the pier 'to meet the boat'. It was a ritual born out of the uniformity of daily life; it didn't

122

matter that there was no visitor to meet or any item to collect – there were new faces to see even if they were only hanging over the railings as their wearers waited for the boat to chug on to its next port of call. 'Meeting the boat' continued to be a Hebridean pastime long after the frontiers of isolation had been demolished by accelerating communications and the years of war.

Those of us who lived 'out of town' soon convinced our relatives to adjust their meal hours to the hours of the Tarbert lodgers so that we could join our schoolmates in the promenade. We would deposit our school satchels in a friendly shop till it was time to take the road up Caw, and we would each join his or her own little pack. Boys and girls never walked together, of course. The girls teetered along in knots of three or four with their heads close together in secret conversation and giggling. The boys, in similar groups, swaggered with hands deep in pockets and shoulders swaying, pretending not to notice the girls unless, occasionally, to challenge them to outrageous and improbable assignations. Every now and again the smokers would melt into an alleyway for a drag, careful to post a look-out for The Blus, who was capable of thrusting his head into the most unexpected corner in search of misdeed. At half past five every day he would stalk down the street to the pier, his tweed cap sedately square over his forehead, swinging his silver-mounted walking stick; occasionally he would stop to exchange a sentence or two with one or two of the more solid citizens but, by and large, his only acknowledgment of the townsfolk was a nod and a grunt. At ten to six he would walk back up the street glancing into shop doors and probing into the occasional alley, and woe-betide the country boy or girl who wasn't off the street by then. He didn't bother about the pupils whose homes were in the town; they were the responsibility of their parents. But his duty, *in loco parentis*, was firmly fulfilled with regard to those of us who had no parents to supervise us. To the best of his ability he was trying to maintain a boarding school regime against some considerable odds. On Sundays he would sit in the aisle seat in the pew he had occupied for years, looking around and checking who was and who wasn't present, and the boy or girl who missed two Sundays in a row could expect to be summoned to his room at four o'clock on Monday. Any excuse had to be backed up by a note from landlady or guardian. Even the inventive third year boy who tried to plead on soul and conscience that he had decided to embrace the Muslim faith was told that he was a member of a free country and could be a Muslim for the five school days provided he stood up in class in front of his fellows and bowed thrice to Mecca; on Saturdays he could be whatever he wanted to be; on Sundays he would be in a pew in either the Church of Scotland or the Free Presbyterian Church. And that was that.

I was fortunate. Big Grandfather's house was a good mile out of town, and then a quarter of a mile down a track towards the seashore. Once there I could range the countryside with impunity provided I avoided the loch which The Blus occasionally fished for trout, and kept well clear of the main road along which he took frequent evening constitutionals. I got to know every sheeptrack on the shore crofts and I could follow them and even on the brightest autumn evening could reach Wee Grandfather's house without fear of detection. Once there, in the company of my cousin, life was my own. Together he and I fished the moorland lochs and streams to our hearts' content and, as the nights got longer and the trout got fewer, we visited the houses where we knew the locals met to exchange yarns and the news of the day. There was a whole enclave of my father's people still living round the bay to which their ancestors had been evicted from the Southlands long ago, a few of them still living in little black houses like the one that Old Hector lived in back home. They were all great story-tellers on my father's side, and the wireless had not yet killed out the pastime romanticised as *ceilidhing*. There is a deep-rooted conviction that Hebrideans spent (nay, spend) their evenings congregated round peat fires in selected houses drinking drams and singing Gaelic songs. Not in that part of the world. Not now. Not then. They congregated, for sure, if four or five comprised a congregation, but it was to talk of the times and the news of the world and occasionally to recall an old story with nary a dram in sight save at a wedding or, sometimes, at a wake. The talk was an education in itself, but not, necessarily, the form of education in which The Blus put his faith, nor the kind that my father fondly imagined I was imbibing. Big Grandfather didn't have my father's pre-occu-

124

pation with book-learning; his concern was with my physical well-fare and, if the evening was fine and the night not too dark, the only stipulation he made was that I should be home by ten. If he saw me, between then and bedtime, attempting to rush through a piece of school homework by the light of the hissing Tilley lamp – the brand new evaporating paraffin lamp which burnt a brilliant gauze filter, and which was beginning to supplant the yellow glowing old oil lamps in the more modern homes – he discouraged me lest I might strain my eyes. And Wee Grandmother would back him up with a quotation from the Bible to the effect that 'much reading was a weariness to the flesh'. The result was that most of my study was done in my little attic room by the light of a candle which I lit as soon as I heard Grandfather draw his first snore.

On Saturday night everybody went to town – everybody, that is, who was under middle age and unsmitten by matrimony or religion. Some of the older married men might make their ways to the pub for a couple of quiet pints and then adjourn to the cobbler's shop for an hour or two of conversation and discussion of community affairs but, by and large, family men and people of Big Grandfather's vintage spent the evening at home preparing for the Sabbath. Grandfather would do the milking, redd out the byre and the outhouses, and bring in four pails of spring water to supply the kitchen till Monday morning: although he now had a bathroom and running taps all the water for cooking and drinking was drawn from the cool, stone-lined well which had been dug and bottomed with filtering gravel by his father or, maybe, somebody long before that. When his chores were over he would betake himself to the bathroom and spend half an hour meticulously stropping his two beautiful Sheffield steel open razors; when they were so sharp that they would slice a hair dangling from his forefinger and thumb he would return one to its box and give himself a slow close shave with the other; he used his razors week about, maintaining that good steel rejuvenated itself if it was given rest. That was the last act of his 'working' week; cleaned and spruced he would make his way to his big mahogany chair in the living room, put on his gold spectacles and settle down to an hour with the *Stornoway Gazette*. Grannie, having completed her housework till every dish was tidily in the dresser, and the

125

table set for Sunday breakfast, would wind the aged pendulum clock which had ticked its way through her long married life, and then she would put on her tortoise shell glasses and ease herself into the Taransay chair across the fire from her man, clutching some church magazine. Thus, peacefully and with the orderliness of years, their week drew gently to its close. For them the nights of going to the town were over.

Three roads converged in town. One from the south which passed the end of Grandfather's croft road, one from the west that threaded through a few hamlets before beginning to claw its lonely way up through the moors and over the towering Clisham on its way to Stornoway which was a real town, or so they said, with gas-light on its streets and a picture house instead of our cobbler's shop; the third road was a short gravel track, barely passable by car, which ended after a few miles eastwards in the tiny shore village of Kyles Scalpay. The communities living along those three roads not only had their own individual existences, they had their own inter-connections forming, as it were, three separate communes with their own distinctive characteristics. Only special occasions drew them together – like shearing or Sundays or Saturday nights. From the top of the hill above Caw where we boys sometimes congregated before descending to the town we could see the trickles of people from the three directions making their ways to town. The older men – older but still on the right side of middle age – wore their best suits and walked singly or in twos with the confidence of many Saturdays. The younger ones (our heroes) sported Harris Tweed jackets and grey flannels; there was an eagerness in their walk and a recklessness if they were on bicycles, and we knew that when we tagged on to them later on they would be smelling of beer and brilliantine. The girls walked in giggles of three or four and where they went we knew not because, in those days, only the most brazen hussy would go into the hotel and none at all into the pub. Most probably they collected in the kitchens of the big houses where sisters or cousins would be in service, or in the houses of friends, from which they would emerge after pub closing time for a discreet promenade – for an assignation, or in hope.

For us there was no point in rushing into town; we were too

young for anything worthwhile, and it was only after the pub skailed that the 'action' would begin and even then our pleasures would be vicarious. But, in due course, we scrambled down the hillside on to the main road and made our way into town anyway, just as the older night-outers melted into their various haunts and as our schoolmates emerged from their lodgings. In actual fact the first part of evening would be just a repeat of our normal après-school round except that it had the subtle excitement of Saturday, of the descending dark and the gentle fluorescing of lights in the windows of those shops whose owners were worldly enough to squeeze the last drips of profit out of the last hours before the Sabbath. They were invariably the ones who would be exchanging their crouch behind the tills for an upright stance behind the collection plate in one or other of the kirks tomorrow. Except for Ali, of course. His God was away on the dark side of the world, and since Ali hadn't as yet attached himself to either of the Tarbert churches there were no taboos for him to offend, and his shop could glow to within minutes of the midnight hour. And it glowed much brighter than the rest.

Ali had come to Harris as a packman several years before but, unlike his fellows who came and left with the swallows, he had decided, for some reason best known to himself, to settle down in our peat and heather island. Wicked rumour had it that he had decided to put several oceans between himself and a wife and scroosh of children but that was disproved to everybody's satisfaction – if slight surprise – when he elected to marry one of the most desirable young women in the community. In many another Scottish society in that age that would have been a sensational happening, but the Harrisman can be periodically pragmatic and within a very short space of time Ali and his bride had settled into a comfortable little house at the neck of the pier. He had discarded his pack and opened up a little shop in which he sold silks and satins and lotions and potions which were exotic by the standards of the established stores. He had a flair for display and, in the lamplight especially, his window glittered as if it were eternal Christmas. Bottles of eau de Cologne rubbed shoulders with improbably coloured bath salts which made discreet claims to ease rheumatism; bright red packets of Craven A cork-tipped cigarettes were stacked in pyramids and draped with silk handkerchiefs to suggest that the man who smoked Craven A had style; he reversed the usual trend of things by having scintillating beads on display for the white natives; there was an assortment of brilliantines and hair oils and pomades that turned schoolboy heads as we pressed up against his window with our manes sleeked back with God's good water. And other things besides.

'I bet you he's got French letters,' said a fellow on third year who knew a thing or two. He spoke in Gaelic with a bravado meant to impress the raw recruits from the country.

'Yes, plenty galore,' shouted Ali from behind the window in Gaelic only faintly tinged with Eastern blemish. 'You come in. You see!' he went on in English, bending down to pull a drawer on to the counter. 'Hurry up before Blus come!' He gave an imperious sideways flick of his head as he saw us hesitating. The very mention of The Blus was enough to galvanise us into some sort of action even in such an improbable situation; there were only two courses of action we could take, so we began to shuffle in – each one trying not to be first through the door and yet with an urgency of curiosity in our jostle. We ended up in a tight knot of five on one side of the counter with Ali, looking for all the world like a magician on the point of producing a rabbit, guddling in the drawer. And with a conjurer's flourish he produced a pink envelope.

'Look!' he said. 'A pack of three. One shilling.'

We looked and shuffled and said nothing.

Very deliberately he opened the envelope and produced a flat rubber medallion which he proceeded, very carefully, to unroll on to the second finger of his left hand. One was aware of heavy breathing all round, and an occasional gulp.

'You put on like this,' he said holding up the rubber-covered finger like a doctor about to make an unmentionable examination. 'Then you not get girl in trouble. But you not put on *finger* or you get girl in plenty trouble. You know where to put.'

We were all becoming acutely aware where to put, but there seemed to be no intelligent comment that any of us could make. To anybody who had chanced to look through the window the silent frozen tableau would have looked like an obscene postcard. But, fortunately, the street had not yet come to life.

'You buy?' said Ali thrusting an unopened packet towards the fellow who had been so brash outside. Suddenly his self-confidence evaporated.

'N-n-no.' He managed to stammer at last. And then in desperation he flung a shilling on the counter. 'It was a packet of Craven A I wanted.' It was a desperate reaction from the only non-smoker in the company, but it got us off the hook and the prospect of sharing twenty Craven A between five of us compensated for Ali's laughter behind us as we tumbled out of the shop. It was a very chastened Farquhar Angus that we hustled into the nearest alleyway, and it was in vain that he pleaded that that was the last shilling of his pocket money.

By the time we had stamped out the burnt cork tips of our first full cigarette of the evening the public bar of the hotel had begun to skail.

The first to emerge were always the older, stone-cold sober men who wouldn't deign to wait to be hounded out by the landlord's shouts of 'Time!'. They had long since served their apprenticeships – some of them in bars far, far afield – and they threw back their nips and sipped their pints for pleasure, not for kicks. If there was anything to show that they had imbibed at all it was that they walked just a shade more sedately than before and by the time they had a ritual run-off against the wall behind Duncan's store they would be ready for an hour of serious discussion with their peers who had forsaken the bar completely as their youth had forsaken them, and had taken to making their only rendezvous the cobbler's little shop. The men with the beer on their breath would push their way in through the pipe-smoke, bringing with them new subjects for conversation. After their contributions had been analysed and discussed for a while somebody would glance at the ancient time-piece on the wall and say 'Which way is the clock?' and after a consultation of fob watches it would be decided whether it was fast or slow and, regardless of which, they would file slowly homewards secure in the knowledge that their heads and their consciences would be clear come the chiming of the church bell in the morning.

The brilliantine boys were different altogether. They would erupt from the pub in an exuberance of high spirits just a moment or two before they were due to be ejected. They would stagger to their bicycles with half bottle bulges on their breasts

129

and screwtops of beer protruding from their hips. For them, optimistically, the best was yet to come as the young women – as if by coincidence – emerged from their places of visit. This was the highlight of the evening that we cockerels had waited for; this was where our longings became our vicariousness as we watched the teamings up and wondered who had paid a stealthy visit to Ali's shop and who was going to do 'that' to whom – and where? We hovered.

Down where the three roads met there was a wall of sitting height on one side, and on the other a big house with a shadow at the end of it. Since the three roads that led to everywhere met there it was a natural place at which to meet by accident!

'Hello Mary Ann, and are you wanting a cross-bar home?'

Since the fellow making the offer would be in a state of doubt as to whether he was propping the bike or the bike propping him, Mary Ann would be foolish in the extreme to accept the offer even if other doubts weren't put into her mind.

'Don't be daft, Mary Ann, it's more than a cross-bar you'll be getting if you go with him!'

'You'd fare better with Geordie Allan; the last time he gave Peggy Jean MacKenzie a cross-bar she was half way across the Huisinis road when she discovered it was a lady's bike he was riding.'

The ribaldry was fast and furious and the boyos from the pub in such effervescent form that a remark about the weather was good for a laugh. But it was the quiet ones that we watched – the couples who would slip into the shadow of the big house, whisper for a few moments, and slip off silently hand in hand. We would pick on a pair and stalk them carefully in the hope of catching them in the act which our salacity convinced us they were planning; but they had been at the game themselves and easily gave us the slip, or else they would ambush us and the fellow would give us a cuffing for our pains. Some of the bolder of us would hang about on the fringe of the crowd hoping for pickings in the shape of some plump teenager with a 'reputation'. But it never worked out that way and as the night wore on the assembly dissolved as couples paired and vanished, or the swains who had imbibed too freely sicked up their week's savings over the wall and set off ignominiously alone, wheeling their bikes erratically beside them. At last we'd be alone with our frustrations and our imaginings, and nothing left to do but trudge back home hoping for better luck next Saturday. My cousin and I walked the south road together.

'Boy, if only I'd got near the doctor's servant I'd have made it for sure. She's got tits like footballs, and she kept looking at me ...'

I had heard it all before. He had some peculiar obsession with the doctor's maids; I'd heard him boasting about three of them, and had long since ceased believing him. In any case, by the time we reached the end of Big Grandfather's road my ardour would have subsided in the face of the prospect that I wouldn't be home in time for prayers. And on a Saturday night that would have been sin. Almost always I made it just as the pendulum clock struck half past ten; rarely did my lateness merit more than a pale stare over the top of my grandfather's gold spectacles. My oatcakes and milk would be sitting on a corner of the table alongside tomorrow's breakfast dishes.

'Anything fresh in town, boy?'

'No. Nothing at all.'

I would eat my supper in silence, with a strange home-longing coming over me as I listened to the aged clock wearily measuring time; no other sound except for an occasional sigh from my grandmother as she came across some reference that reminded her of the frailty of mortality – something which always weighed on her more heavily than usual on Saturday nights and Sundays. When Grandfather saw me picking up my dishes to carry them to the scullery he would begin to put away his paper and reach for the big Bible, and Grannie would tuck the *Christian Herald* or *The Witness* (as she still insisted on calling the church magazine although it had long since changed its name) below the cushion of her chair. By the time I had rinsed my cup and plate below the tap the old man would have the Bible open on his knee and he'd be polishing his spectacles, ready to bring down the curtain on another week.

And so, the routine went on as autumn gave way to winter.

For the first few days of term I had missed the village, and although a little attic room all to myself was an escape from the crowded little house in the Southlands, and a bathroom with running hot water a sophistication beyond my dreams, there had still been an emptiness in being plucked out of a large warm family like a kitten suddenly sold from a litter. But as I began to find my feet in my new environment and get to know my way around in town my attitudes began to change. The loneliness gave way to a sense of freedom; it was marvellous never to be called on to do chores any more but be waited on, hand and foot, by Grandmother; the more I got into the swing of the gentlemanly life the better I liked it, and the company I kept was infinitely more swanky than the horny-handed men in the village and the bare-foot boys and girls of Primary School with darns in their jerseys. It was only on Saturday nights now that little twinges of that home-longing returned, but they would dispel when I got up to the attic room; I had discovered that I could smoke with impunity in my own room, once my grandparents were in bed, so long as I kept the skylight open a crack and made sure that the douts rolled down the slates into the guttering. I kept a copy of *The Pilgrim's Progress* and *The Works of Robert Louis Stevenson* beside my bed but, tucked in among my clothes, I had a store of lurid paperbacks from the mildly pornographic library which circulated surreptitiously from hand to hand below the desk lids in school. Propped up in bed with one of those and a glowing Woodbine the feeling of the good life quickly returned.

Every week since the very beginning of term I had received a letter from my mother by Tuesday morning's post enclosing two shillings carefully wrapped in newspaper because it was reckoned to be illegal to send coins through the post; but the two shillings must have strained her resources sufficiently without having to lay out the poundage charge on a postal order. At first, her bits and pieces of news were read and re-read with avid interest and when, in mid-September, she added a post-script saying 'I nearly forgot to tell you that Old Hector is going to get married ...' I wrote back immediately demanding to know more. She replied saying, '... they say she's a woman from Uist, but nobody knows for sure and nobody knows how he met her. I hope she's nice, but your father says that she must be wrong in the head to be marrying Hector but that isn't right. Hector's a very kind man, but if it's Uist she's from it'll be in Uist the wedding will be ...'

And so it was. Three weeks later she wrote to say that Hector had been quietly married in Uist and that his bride was, indeed, 'a nice, homely woman'. But by that time the world of Old Hector and the world of the village seemed a long way away and not so very important. My mother's letters were fast losing their interest too. They seemed to consist of catalogues of unimportant things like the price of heifers at sales, a pick-up in the Harris Tweed market, somebody expecting yet another baby, and all the other trivia of small village life. She was also allowing an irritating nag to creep into the correspondence. '... we're glad you caught twelve trout last week, but your father says that you must be sure to do your homework in the evening ...' or '... we're sure it was very exciting in Tarbert on Saturday night with Alex John MacRae getting drunk, and it's only right that you should enjoy yourself, but remember that it's quite a strain keeping you in high school so that you get a better chance than poor Alex John ever had, and we hope that you're doing well at your lessons ...'

Now we were well into bleak December and another week was over. Heavy rain had cast a gloom on the Saturday safari but even if the doctor's maid had made the most generous offer imaginable I doubt whether I could have summoned up the enthusiasm to take advantage of it. If there had been an alternative to a Saturday night alone with my grandparents I doubt whether I'd have gone to town at all. As it was I'd come back home as early as I dared do without risking questions from the old folk; I had had my supper and knelt through prayers that seemed even longer than usual and now, at last, I was safely in my room with a tasteless cigarette in my lips. For the umpteenth time I was reading through my school end-of-term report card with which The Blus had eventually presented me – after a half-hour session in his room on the previous evening, with the warning that it was to be taken home to my parents when I went back to the village for the Christmas break, and that it was to be brought back signed personally by my father. I had read and re-read the column of subject and marks but, always, my eyes returned to the last line. *Place in class – 32. Number in class 32.*

In two days' time I'd be going back to the village for my first holiday from High School. And meeting my father.

Chapter Ten

It was a strange feeling, to be returning to one's own home on holiday; it was made stranger still by the burden of apprehension and guilt that weighed in on me as I stood waiting for the bus at the red gate. My suitcase was heavy with the weight of cake and black pudding and freshly killed mutton that my grandparents were sending to my mother to supplement the Christmas table, and I had a parcel of hand-me-down jumpers and cardigans from an aunt who was married to a merchant and could afford to indulge her flair for style; packed in among the knitwear were an assortment of little packages which I guessed contained toys for my brothers' Christmas stocking and probably a pipe and pipe tobacco for my father. I was laden, in fact, with everything that would make for good cheer except good news. Deep down I hoped that my father would explode; I could stand that better than his tight silence and the deep hurt that could show in his eyes.

The bus was crowded. There were merchant navy men coming home for Christmas and New Year leave and it was obvious that they had already started celebrating; there were glamorous young ladies home on holiday from nursing or service in Glasgow; there was the usual hard core of men from the Southlands who had come north by the morning bus and were now on their way back home smelling of tweed and beer; and there were the three 'scholars' from my own village whom I knew to have fared well in their first term exams. All of those had one thing in common; they had something to feel happy about. For me it was a long and dreary journey, aggravated by the fact that I had to pretend good cheer and join the general bonhomie. The bus seemed to stop at every homestead between Tarbert and the new village before it finally drew up at the gate to my home. As I stepped off and took my heavy case from Jackie the driver who heaved it on to the running board for me, I could see my father coming down towards the road from the byre. I guessed that he had been hovering there, pretending to be doing odd jobs rather than be at his loom, so that he could keep a weather eye open for the bus coming over the Back of Scarista hill.

'Hullo my boy,' he said, offering his hand as he hefted my case with the other. 'It's grand having you back home with us again. And, Good Lord, I think you've put on a couple of inches in height; I'm having to look up to you already. O, and here's herself; she's been like a hen on a hot griddle since morning, and she'd have had me kill the fatted calf if there had been a fatted calf to kill.' My mother was standing at the door, wiping her hands on her apron. For a second I thought she was going to kiss me but she settled for squeezing my arm instead. 'You're looking well,' she said. 'Your grandmother's cooking must be agreeing with you; I'm afraid you'll be finding your poor mother's efforts a bit wishy-washy after all the fine fare in Dieraclate!' I knew by the smell from the stove that that was unlikely to be the case; the first whiff told me that some cockerel or hen had come to an untimely end.

'Grannie sent some mutton and black puddings and things; they're in my case. And there's a parcel from Auntie Mary; it's got clothes in it for you and Christmas presents for the boys.'

My three brothers, sitting in a row on St Clement's bench, merely wriggled their bottoms where they sat. The whole atmosphere was peculiarly unreal because the situation was totally new; never before had a member of the family been away from home for three and a half months, and, suddenly a strange gulf divided us. I was conscious that I was dressed much better than any of the rest; whatever I might have to say to my brothers later, there was nothing that I could think of to say to them in public. But above all else I felt uncomfortable because of the tininess of the room. It had been my home since boyhood, and I had known little but happiness there even during the years of our poverty. But now, after the spaciousness of Big Grandfather's house, it seemed claustrophobic and – truth to tell – a little dingy and hovelly. My father guessed my thoughts.

'You'll be finding us a bit humble after the fine lodgings you've had. But never mind, boy – when you're finished at University with an M.A. and making a great name for yourself you'll be able to send us enough money to build a grand white house that will put Dieraclate in the shade.'

'Not at all,' said my mother. 'He'll be marrying a toff from the mainland as soon as he qualifies and we'll be lucky if he comes back for a week to the Rodel Hotel! But what's all this nonsense about anyway? Sit down there and let's see what you've got in your case and I'll get on with setting the table.'

The mention of marriage made my brothers laugh, and the atmosphere relaxed at last. I sat down beside them on the settle and began to open Auntie Mary's parcel and distribute her presents even though she had given strict instructions for the smaller packages to be left unopened till Christmas. By the time the meal was on the table conversation was flowing in torrents – my parents trying to enquire after relatives and about the excitements of Tarbert while my brothers talked each other down in the eagerness of each to be first with the news of school and the village.

Mother had always been a good cook and had managed to conjure up meals out of nothing during the Depression years, but she had really pulled all the stops out for my welcome home. Three courses, and tea and biscuits to round off. It was the sort of spread that one associated with weddings or Communion times.

'Well, well,' said my father as he pushed back his chair and felt for his pipe. 'I reckon we'll have to arrange for you to come home two or three times a term if it's going to mean a dinner like that.'

'Listen to him!' My mother was obviously flattered by his compliment. 'I slave over that stove for half my life and he never even notices what I put down in front of him.'

'And now some cheery news to round it all off, eh?' Father

had his pipe going. 'How's school coming along? How did the tests go?'

'I've got a report card you've to sign and send back to the Headmaster.'

I could feel my throat constricting and my voice sounded a whole tone higher; I sensed rather than saw a suspicious look coming into his eyes as I left the table and dug in my case for the buff envelope. I handed it to him without a word. My mother looked from me to him. My brothers felt there was something amiss and fell silent, staring at my father as he scanned the card. I could see his jaw muscle tightening as he clenched his pipe, and I saw his eyes move back to the top of the card as if he couldn't believe what he had read the first time. At last he laid the card on the table and took the pipe from his mouth.

'Well, by God, I suspected that something was wrong from the skimpy things that you chose to call letters when you deigned to send them. But not for a minute did I imagine anything like this –'

'John! What's wrong?'

'Wrong? I'll tell you what's wrong. Our bloody son has humiliated us in front of the whole of the goddamned island –'

'Watch your language in front of the children!'

'The children are going to hear every word I've got to say about the clown of a brother they've got. Our big man who parades the Tarbert street on a Saturday night as if he was God Almighty from what I hear. Our great fisherman who catches more trout than the landlord. Our nancy-boy who looked as if he had walked into a tinker's camp when he came in through that door. He has come *last* in his class – that's what he's done! He's come bloody last in a class that I happen to know contains a couple of the biggest dim-wits in Tarbert!' He turned on me with an anger in his eyes that I had never seen before – a steely, cold anger. 'I put all my hopes in you. I taught you everything I knew myself although God knows that wasn't much – I didn't have bursaries and daft parents to buy books for me. And you've thrown it all back in my face like a shovel of shit. What were you up to? Boozing, or smoking your lungs out, or trying to get below the skirts of every tarty servant girl in Tarbert?'

'John!'

'No! I'll not stop till I've had my say. And that's not much now. I stood by you, lad, when you failed to get the bursary the first time because I knew you had tried and nobody can do more than that. But now it's all I can do to keep my hands off you. Not just for my sake, but for your mother's. She's slaved for you; she's put money past herself when she hardly had clothes to put on her own back so that you could go to High School dressed like a gentleman. And what has she got in exchange? Humiliation in her native village, in front of her own people.'

He stopped and held my eyes.

'What have you got to say for yourself?'

There was nothing I could say.

'Nothing! Just as I thought! Well I've got one thing to say, and then I'm saying no more. I'm giving you till summer in Tarbert school and if, by that time, you're not in the first five places in that class you're going to come back home here and sit at that loom weaving tweed till you've got more calluses on your backside than all of your forefathers had corns on their feet. And that's my last word on it!'

And it was. He lit his pipe with a slight shake in his hand, picked up the *Daily Express*, which he hadn't opened since the bus driver left it tucked into the handle of my suitcase, and withdrew into a chilly concentration.

One by one my brothers slipped away from the table. My mother sat for a few moments staring down at her plate, and then stood up.

'I'd better get on with washing those dishes.'

It wasn't meant but that one sentence stung more than all of my father's wrath. The weariness in her tone conveyed her disappointment, and the reference to the dishes reminded me of all the trouble she had gone to in order to make me welcome back home.

'I'll dry for you.'

'No. You've got your good suit on.'

I got up and went over to St Clement's bench and sat silently wondering what I could do to occupy myself. I could think of nothing. And just sat. My father didn't say another word; nor ever again did he refer to the report card – not even when he handed it back to me, signed.

I don't know how the evening would have dragged on if my mother hadn't taken matters into her own hands. When she was lighting the lamp she turned to me – not with a smile but with a hint of sympathy in her voice. 'O Finlay, I nearly forgot … I met Old Hector last night and I swore to him that I would get you to call in on him tonight. His wife's called Catriona, by the way. She's a really nice woman.' I could have hugged mother for getting me out of the ice-box situation and I had to restrain myself from running out of the room.

When the cold air hit me I realised that I was bursting for a pee and, momentarily, I checked my step as I thought of going to the bathroom. But in the same split instant I remembered there wasn't one. As I stood relieving myself against the back wall of the house my resentment of earlier on surfaced momentarily as I realised that, for the next fortnight, I would be reverting to the old modes of life. No running water. No room of my own. No toilet and toilet paper; instead a cold squat on two rocks in a hidden crook of the river. My father was right. I'd have to get on with my school-work or I'd be shitting in the open and washing my face in a bucket for the rest of my life.

It was a new road I walked on the way to Hector's. A cold road. A pallid moon hung over the village and there was a gripe of frost in the air, but that wasn't the cold that I felt. It was a chill of the mind. As I walked past my old Primary School, where I'd been leathered by the sadistic Miss Dalbeith and coached and encouraged by Miss Martin, I realised how very small it was although it had seemed a huge building when I first approached it as a five year old trotting at my father's side. Now it had an unreal 'doll's house' quality about it, and none of the style and grandeur of the big school in the Northlands. It was impossible to believe that I had spent eight years of my life there, and I didn't even remember that I had spent a happy year there even before school began, when, as a family, we had lodged in the living-quarters end of it, sharing accommodation with the Boer War veteran and the Duchess and Molly who had tried to poison me. None of those memories came back as I hurried past lest Miss Martin might still be in residence and would pop out to ask me about the fulfilment of my promise in my new posh school. I had been one of her star pupils according to herself once, and thirty-second out of thirty-two would not sound exactly like the crowning of her ambitions for me.

It wasn't just the school that looked small. The village itself seemed to have shrunk and lost that burgeoning promise that it had clung to during the ten years since my parents and their neighbours had come and founded it in the confidence that they had reached their land of milk and honey. It had survived its growing pains as the pioneers made their mistakes and some strove for too much too soon; it survived the Depression when the natural resources of its sea and countryside saved it from the deprivation that beset the cities. It had heard the laughter of my boyhood generation. Now it was just a tired straggle of houses along a gravel road with the wind from the sea beginning to turn the crispness of the frost to damp. Our own corrugated iron shack out of which, by my father's mismanagement as I judged it in my present mood, we had never graduated, looked like a symbol of eternal poverty rather than the cosy family nest it had once been. There's something different about the village, I thought. Something has happened to it. But I didn't have the wits to see that the something was happening to me.

Time took a step backwards as I reached Old Hector's thatched black house. There it stood, with its two little windows recessed into its six foot thick walls and its roof of layered marram grass, like an old man with his bonnet pulled over his eyes. Whatever else had changed it hadn't. It stood now as it had stood when my Great Aunt Rachel was a girl and it had been old then. It had seen populations come and go, but it had crouched there in its timelessness untouched by any passing whim of society and untempted into the new age of amenity. I didn't think all that out as I stood there, of course. I didn't think of anything. But my depression and my mood of grudge melted away. I approached the door as if my last visit had been yesterday.

But something had changed – dramatically. The door opened as I reached it and I was greeted by a big strong woman with rosy cheeks and a twinkle that made one smile.

'Come in,' she said. 'I know who you are and I know all about you. Himself here was just wondering if you'd be along to see us. Maybe he'll be too grand now he was saying; but I knew you wouldn't be if you were the kind of fellow he had told me about!'

While she was talking she ushered me into the crouched old living room that I knew so well, but I wouldn't have known it now if somebody had put me inside, blindfold, and then uncovered my eyes. The gloom had disappeared. The peat-fire burnt brightly on the hearth; the interior stone walls had been white-washed so that they reflected the light from the oil-lamp and would do the same to the light from the deep little window in the daytime; there was a general impression of airiness and freshness, flecked here and there with chintzes of predominant reds and yellows. It was an incredible transformation and it was all I could do not to stand and gawp. But there was a greater transformation still. The old Taransay chair had been stripped of its layers of brown paint and varnish and repainted white; and, cushioned in it, was Old Hector in a clean shirt such as he had hitherto worn only for church or for funeral … and once, long ago, at the Christmas Treat. Beside him on a little table improvised from a three-legged milking stool were laid out his pipe, paper spills, a short rope of bogey roll and a knife for slicing it. This was the man who had been used all his life to being sent out to the end of the house for a smoke if his sister Maggie happened to be in bad form. The enormity of what I had done last mid-summer flashed through my mind as I remembered that advertisement which read *Retired seaman wants woman used to croft work with a view to matrumony. Reply Box 427.* Yet here was the outcome of it all – success by all appearances.

'You sit down there beside Hector while I dash out to the well for a fresh pail of water, and then we'll have a wee cup of tea.'

She placed a chair beside Hector's while he pumped my hand with both of his. He patted the seat of the chair.

'Sit down boy and light up. Catriona is as trusty as myself; she'll not be telling your parents you have a wee puff now and again, will you Catriona?'

'Of course I won't. But I'm not sure that I approve of young boys smoking though; it makes them grow into ugly old men like one I can think of.' She chuckled and went out. As soon as the door swung to behind her the smile went off Old Hector's face; he lent towards me and gripped my arm, and he dropped his voice to a whisper.

'Quick. Listen to me before she comes back. There's only one lie I've ever told her; I told her the advertisement was all my own idea and that it came to me in a dream one night. I – er – well – er – I sort of let her think it was – well – some kind of message from on High … the kind of things that used to happen in the Old Testament. I didn't say it was that, but I sort of hinted at it. Oh! And I told her that she was the only one who replied. It wasn't much of a lie, was it?'

'It was two lies.'

'No it wasn't! I've thought that one out. It was two halves of one!'

I managed to keep my face straight, and pretended to be thinking out my attitude. His grip on my arm tightened.

'It wasn't much more of a deceit than not telling the truth about smoking, was it?'

The old blackmailer! I was glad that he hadn't changed too much after all.

'Ach no,' I said. 'And it isn't all that far from being the truth anyway.'

He relaxed.

'Do you know what she calls me when we're on our own?' He paused, and I shook my head. 'Four-two-seven! That's what she calls me.' He slapped his knee and, for the first time, I heard the old man laugh out loud. The old man? Somehow he didn't seem old any more. He lent towards me again. 'There's one thing; she's a wee bit too old to be having children; may be we should have put an age limit in the paper, eh?'

'Then Catriona wouldn't have replied.'

'Dammit man, that's what education does for you! I never thought of that.' He was still chuckling as Catriona came back from the well.

'And how are you getting on with Primrose?' I asked as we sat over tea and scones. 'Is she milking as well as ever?'

'Better, my boy. Better.' said Hector.

'And it's not just Primrose any more,' the new wife continued, and I noticed how effortlessly she took the conversation out of Hector's hands. 'I had a cow of my own and I brought her with me, and she and Primrose are both in

142

calf. We're thinking we'll keep one of the calves for rearing, if there's a female one, and sell the other with calf at foot.' It struck me that Hector hadn't only got himself a wife but a manageress into the bargain – a manageress with a cow at foot. The business of bringing on a new calf of good strain to be a milking cow was sound common sense, but I couldn't help hoping that Primrose would be the one to drop the female calf and thus be the one to stay. After all, but for Primrose that advertisement would never have been written.

The visit was long and late, and the moon had shrunk behind the haar when Old Hector accompanied me to the door. He had picked up a torch from the window sill as he passed.

'I'll walk you a bit down the path,' he said. 'Catriona tells me that those bandy legs of mine need exercise, and may be she's got a point.' I was going to expostulate but he stopped me. 'No, no. I'll be all right. And besides I want a yarn with you.'

We walked in silence for a while – and slowly because Hector's feet were bad.

'So school didn't go so well, then?'

I stopped dead.

'What do you mean? How do you know?'

'Ach, I've known you a long time. I've watched you growing up. When you're a bit of an oddity like me – whether it's bad legs or timidity or whatever – people let their guards down and reveal more of themselves than they would normally do to what they would think of as a whole man. And so I've seen more of you than even your parents have done; I've seen the deeper you where they've been concerned with other things – like your welfare, and your health, and your education and so on. But I learnt to read your eyes. Just after you came into the house I said something about what education does for a man and a cloud came over your eyes which told me everything. What went wrong?'

I told him everything – the disastrous examination results and my father's outburst. He listened without interrupting, except to touch my arm and make me resume our slow walk down the path beside the churchyard. When I finished he stopped again.

'As you know, my boy, I never got much in the way of

education, and even if I had done I'm not sure that I'd have known what to do with it. I've never worried about it. But your father's different; he's a clever man and if he'd had the chance the Lord only knows how he'd have ended up. But because he's intelligent enough to know what he missed he allowed a tiny little bit of bitterness to sow itself somewhere; perhaps he had too much time to think in that kind of war that he had. And a seed like that creates a canker in your mind just as a thorn in your thumb can cause an abscess. But then you came along and it so happens that you developed the same sort of interests as he had, and it was like a cure for him. He began to see all the things that he had hoped for for himself being fulfilled in you; and he thinks you've not only let him down but you've destroyed his hopes … and that's the worst thing you can do to a man. He'll come round when you begin to do better –'

'*If* I do better.'

Hector chortled and took a moment to light his cutty.

'You bloody well will – if only because you can't be thirty-third out of thirty-two!'

He became serious again.

'It's a difficult thing to be chucked into a brand new world. I remember that one and only trip of mine to Singapore … my God boy, nobody knows the half of it. I'd never been out of this village before, and even at home I'd always been in the shadow of my sister Maggie over there,' he nodded towards the grave-yard as casually as if she was standing a few feet away from us in the life, 'and when I got aboard ship I went wild. I had my freedom at last. I was loose in a shining new world where everything was better and bigger than it was here. I've never told you about some of the ports we called into on the way, and what I got up to. And I never will … But I'll tell you this – that bout of malaria that buggered up my legs was what saved my life. It stopped me dead in my tracks. And when I came home here, I made up my mind that I was never going to leave again and never again going to rush. That bad mark is your malaria; it's stopped you dead in your tracks, but, unlike me, you'll get moving again. Only remember this – don't go trying to start from a point out there. Start from here. Your education is out there, but this is where wisdom is. A tree grows from its roots – not from its highest branch, and roots aren't posh and glittery things; they're busy grubbing around in the soil and drawing the goodness from it that will eventually produce the blossom. That's all I'm going to say.'

And I could sense that it was. There was nothing I could say in response so I changed the subject.

'Isn't the beach quiet and empty? That's one thing I miss in the Northlands – the beach!'

He looked out towards the sea for a long time.

'Yes,' he said. 'The beach is quiet and empty but not for long, I'm afraid.'

'What do you mean?'

'I've been reading the papers a lot those last few weeks; Catriona keeps me supplied with them; she says they keep me from getting in her way. And I'll be surprised if we see the next year out without a war. I remember the last one. That beach down there was cluttered from end to end with flotsam that you've never seen the like of. Yes, and a body or two forbye. It was only when the bodies came that it was brought home to us that the sea casts up only what the sea has taken in the first place. And if it was bad last time, what will it be like next time with all the instruments of war they've been inventing while we've been thinking peace … Ach well …' He paused, and then pulled himself together with a visible jerk. 'Goodnight boy; Catriona will be getting worried.' And he turned on his heel and hirpled off up the path, following the spot of his torch. I stared after him in disbelief. It used to be a standing joke in the village that the only things Old Hector feared more than his sister Maggie were the dark and the churchyard at night. Yet there he was – oblivious to them both, and, come to think of it, to Maggie as well. Catriona was obviously a mighty powerful influence in her own twinkly way.

My father was alone in the living room when I got in, checking, as he had done every night of his life, that there was not the remotest chance of a live ember escaping from the dying stove. I felt a sag of relief when he turned round and smiled, and truth to tell, a prickling behind the eyes.

'Did you have a good evening? It was long enough anyway.'

There was no reproach in his voice, and it was obvious that he had been meaning to go to bed and leave the door open for me – something which he had never done before; it was a

145

gesture of confidence which meant infinitely more than words.

'I had a great time. Catriona's very nice isn't she?'

'She's a fantastic woman; she's made a man of Hector in his middle age.' He picked the Bible off the table and returned it to its shelf. 'But how the devil did you talk Hector into putting that advert into the *Gazette*?'

I felt my jaw slackening and it took me all my time not to flop down on the bed that my mother had made up for me on St Clement's bench.

'Who … how … what …?'

'Don't worry. I'm the only one who knows. But then not even the teacher ever seemed to notice that you could never spell matrimony; and the damn fool editor of the *Gazette* obviously didn't notice either.'

He was chortling as he went through to the bedroom. And suddenly it felt as if the Christmas holidays weren't going to be so bad after all.

Chapter Eleven

Winter doesn't really begin till January in the Hebrides. There are November gales and scythings of frost in December and rain anytime, but it isn't till January that the earth has drunk its fill and become so water-logged that even the high ground squelches. Nowadays, modern houses with double glazing and central heating and airing-cupboards have taken the ultimate discomfort out of the pervasive damp but, in those days, even in Big Grandfather's well-fired, bathroomed house, the first three months of the year were dispiriting. Every day, from Monday till Friday, I walked the mile and a half between school and home four times a day – morning and night and each way each day at lunchtime; if I took the short-cut diagonally across Angus Donald Og's croft I had to pick my way through peatland and spongey sphagnum moss, and, sooner or later, a false step would lead to a water-logged boot about which I could do nothing except walk fast or run till the water warmed to body-heat, and, in class when it got cold, wiggle to bring it back to warmth again. If I took the gravel path to the main road then the sodden rushes drooping across the track whipped at my flannel trouser legs and there was nothing for it except to reconcile myself to the feeling of walking around as if my legs were lagged with cold porridge. Even if my father's ultimatum weren't still nagging at me, the thought of changing into dry clothes and going out again at night in order to get drenched afresh would have been enough to stem my ardour for the gallivant.

There is a certain limit to the amount of conversational tapestry that one can weave out of the three strands of God, the sheepstock, and the events of day in school – particularly when the interests of the three parties involved are fairly definitely defined. And so, as soon as the evening meal was over, I tended to head upstairs to my attic and try to muster some enthusiasm for my schoolwork. I found it hard to become addicted to Latin; mathematics and science froze my soul, but I found a new interest in learning to read and write my own native Gaelic for the first time, and, concurrently my old interest in English began to rekindle. I began to delve into the leather-bound volume of Robert Louis Stevenson's works which had lain unopened by my bedside for the whole of first term. I ploughed my way stolidly through the first few pages of *Kidnapped*, there is nothing more difficult than getting into the rhythm of good writing when one has been immersed in trash for a while, but I perservered and by the time David Balfour had recovered consciousness in the bowels of the brig *Covenant* I was in thrall. *Treasure Island* came next and I revelled in its bounding adventure. And then *The Body Snatcher*. It was on a blustery night when the skylight was rattling enough to make me jittery anyway that, after a long straight read, I came to the untying of the sack and the *light falling clear upon the dark well-moulded features and smooth shaven cheeks of a too familiar countenance.* I was glad to rush through the last lines of the story and make for the warmth and the company of downstairs.

The macabre and the supernatural tug at the same nerves and, in the Hebridean of my generation, the belief in the supernatural was submerged only under a very thin veneer of education and sophistication. Big Grandfather was as tough a man as one could meet on a long day's journey; if he met the devil in the dark he would send him on his way. And he had not the faintest doubt that there were more things in heaven and earth than Horatio or anybody else dreamt of. And when he talked of his own experiences in the undefinable realms he was as matter-of-fact as if he were discussing yesterday's most ordinary events. He would have been happier if the eerie light, seen by himself and many people, mysteriously flitting along the edge of craobhag were to fulfil its portent. The craobhag

148

was the high crumbly sea-cliff, with a couple of rowan trees peeping from it, that fell away at the foot of his croft. For generations – once in a while and without warning or possible explanation – a white light would blaze out of nowhere and settle on the top of craobhag momentarily before beginning its restless patrolling along the cliff edge and then plunging into the sea. Grandfather had dreaded all his life that it presaged an accident to one of his own children but they had grown up and gone their ways without mishap. Now his fears were transferred to his grandchildren when they came a-visiting, and I was under strict orders never to go near craobhag edge, and never never at night to the short-cut that ran close to the cliff lest misdirection misguide me towards it. As far as I know the augury of the light has not, so far, been realised. Unlike the other light that I heard grandfather and other people tell of – the light on the white boat.

When he was a young man Big Grandfather, like most of his fellow crofters in the seaside communities, had a sturdy rowing boat which he kept moored at the foot of the croft. He was inordinately proud of his boat – a sixteen foot white skiff which he had bought on the mainland when he gave up a brief career as a seaman and settled down to married life.

In those days, before the arrival of motor transport, a boat was an essential for a sea-side crofter in the Northlands where both terrain and the difficulties of feeding made it impossible to use horses in the way that people in the gentler lands of the south used them. It was only by boat that a man could bring home his sacks of meal or flour, seed corn for sowing or barrels of salt herring for winter. His alternative would be to lug them on his back over miles of rough country. It was by boat that coffins were taken to Rodel churchyard in the south end of the island, since the rocky Northlands couldn't be dug for a cemetery. And a boat, of course, was necessary for fishing in a bay that was sheltered and teeming with fish. Grandfather was inordinately proud of a boat that was acknowledged to be one of the best in the neighbourhood, and he tended her with the meticulous care which he lavished on all the accoutrements of his croft.

Then rumours began to circulate that the white boat was haunted, and people began to be reluctant to work her or travel in her. At first – he admitted in later years – he put it down to mild envy on somebody's part, or even a crafty dodge to make him part with the boat at a knock-down price. Then, suddenly one night, he realised that the rumours, which he had never heard defined, were well founded. He was checking that the front door was closed, prior to going to bed, when he saw what he described as 'a pale light' leaving the white boat and travelling out into the middle of the bay. His first reaction was that poachers had borrowed the boat and he rushed down to the shore to check, only to find that the boat was safely moored as he had left her, while the light was disappearing into the distance on the far side of the bay.

He kept a sporadic look-out thereafter and, on many occasions, he and grandmother saw the light leaving the boat – always at the same late hour – and, from the higher vantage of the house they could watch it move out across the bay and turn gently into the narrow Sound of Scalpay before disappearing behind the headland. And two or three times in the late winter dawn he had seen the light return and slowly extinguish as it reached the mooring. From the beginning he accepted the happening for what he was convinced it was – a foreshadowing of tragedy of some kind … a drowning from the boat, or the loss of the boat itself. People urged him to get rid of her; my grandmother pled with him to sell. But he wouldn't. He maintained, quite simply, that what was predestined would be fulfilled regardless of any effort on his part. In later life, secure in her faith and mellow with experience, she would agree that he had been right and that she had been wrong.

Then, in January 1907 word came that the yacht on which grandfather's brother, Roderick, worked as a deckhand was putting in to anchor in Loch Erisort in Lewis and that Roderick was being allowed home for some days' leave. He never did come. When he and some of his mates were climbing from the yacht into the dinghy taking them ashore the yacht yawed in a sudden squall and swamped the dinghy. Four of the men disappeared. It was late at night when word of the tragedy reached my grandfather and the information that his brother's body was still unrecovered; immediately, he and some of his neighbours set off to join in the search, and, with a lantern in her prow, the white boat moved out into the middle of the bay.

From the window grandmother watched the lantern grow smaller as it reached the Sound of Scalpay and then disappeared round the headland as she had watched that light disappear many times before. She sat up all night waiting and, through the dawn, she saw the white boat rowing back into the bay with the lantern still burning in her stem – and Roderick's body aboard. The light was never seen again, but, a few years later grandfather sold the white boat – not for any reasons of superstition but because she reminded him of a grief.

I had heard the story from other people many times before I heard it from Big Grandfather himself.

'Man,' Grandmother said. 'You'll be giving the boy nightmares – telling him that sort of story; young people nowadays have more on their minds than that sort of thing.'

'But is it true, Grannie?'

'O, it's true all right; I saw the light many times myself although I saw it returning only the once. But things like that don't seem to happen nowadays – or else people don't notice them; they don't have time.'

I suspect that the old lady was near the truth. I caught the tail end of the generation which had time and an uncomplicated attitude to life and belief which made them more receptive – and, perhaps, perceptive. I was aware of the speed of change – one never is when one is at the heart of the vortex; but in that particular year, life in our part of the world was changing dramatically, and perhaps only people like my grandmother, watching from the higher vantage of the years and from a cushioned domesticity, were aware of it. Even Grandfather, when he railed against the increasing difficulties of getting a crew for the cutting of his peat, was inclined to put the problem down to 'laziness of the younger generation' rather than to a change in the social order.

The idea of 'crewing' the peat-cutting was a novelty to me, because it had already died out in the Southlands. It was an elementary form of traditional co-operation which had flourished for years in tight knit communities like those of the Northlands, but was less practicable in a place like our new village where, by virtue of the size of the crofts, people lived farther away from each other, and where, because they were a new community which had come together as strangers, people weren't so inclined to team together. Invariably my father cut his peat over several days of spring with the help of my mother or of a relative. In Dieraclate it was different. The men of the township would assemble on a given evening in late spring and decide on a rota. Then on the allotted day eight or ten of them would arrive with their peat irons and complete one croft's peat-cutting (the whole winter's supply) in one single day. Then, if the next day was fine, they would move on to the next croft; and so on till the peat for the entire village was cut and a few days were added for the widows or the disabled. It was a simple system, and all the more effective because it assumed mildly gala proportions.

Grandfather got up early every day, but particularly early on his own peat-cutting day. It was his responsibility to see that the peat-banks were skinned (the turf removed from the top of the peat proper) and that any collected water was drained away from the trench of the bank. He would lay out his own two cutting irons in case some villager came without one or, for that matter, in case some stranger from another village decided to come along to give a hand just for the joy of a good day out. The remains of last year's peat – such of it as hadn't already been consumed or stacked at the end of the house – had to be cleared back from the spreading area so that the new wet peat had a clear sward. Most of the preparatory work would have been done well before cutting day, but it was mandatory that everything should be checked so that when the men were assembled they would be able to get straight down to work. That was the theory.

While Grandfather was checking the preparation of his own domain, Grandmother was bustling about getting the house in order because she would have up to a dozen people to feed and that involved a lot of organisation even although, in the course of the morning, several village wives would arrive with baskets of home baking and cooked chickens and hunks of cold salt mutton. But these were extras. The onus was still on Grandmother to provide the basic meals so that, even if the neighbours failed to contribute (which was inconceivable), there would still be food to feed the multitude. It would never do to be seen to be beholden; and, devout and all as she was, Grannie preferred to perform her own miracles in advance! In the other years that I could remember, when I had been allowed to go north especially for the peat-cutting if it fell on a Saturday, one of the miracles for me had been Grannie's ashets of seafood. There were oysters in their hundreds down at the foot of the croft where the Yellow Skerry protected a channel of sea from any ruffling of the waters of the bay; and, farther along, below craobhag, there grew gigantic mussels (the size of my cupped hands) which were called 'wolf-mussels'. A pail of oysters and a pail of mussels were collected at the last low tide before the peat-cutting and kept in sea water till morning, when they were boiled till they opened and then rolled in oatmeal and fried. We didn't have oysters or wolf-mussels in the Southlands because the sea was too rough on such patches of rocky shore as we had between the sandy beaches, so Grannie's seafood platters (as the restaurants of later year taught me to call them) were special treats.

'Where are the oysters?' I asked her that beautiful spring morning when, happily for me, Grandfather's crew day had fallen on a Saturday.

'There aren't any this year.'

'Why not?'

'Ask the Good Lord that! I've never known it before. Your grandfather says there isn't a single oyster worth bringing home in the whole of the Yellow Skerry bed.'

'What about the wolf mussels, then? Can't we have them on their own?'

'I'm not chancing them. Chirsty Donald Og picked some a fortnight ago and she and Angus were very sick; she was saying that a couple of people in Caw were ill too, and they're blaming the wolf-mussels. There may be some shellfish disease – I don't know ...'

I didn't know it then, but I was never going to taste a wolf-mussel or a Yellow Skerry oyster again. And neither Grandmother nor I could be expected to associate the mysterious disappearance of the shellfish with the fact that Grandfather's new bathroom was only one of the latest in a whole line of new bathrooms from which pipes led straight into the bay. Not only our beliefs and superstitions were being undermined by the onward skelter of progress.

'Dangitty! People are getting lazier and lazier,' Grandfather muttered for the third or fourth time. 'It's ten o'clock and not a sign of a peat-cutter yet; it's going to be dark by the time we finish – and this a Saturday too!'

'Man of the house,' said Grannie, deliberately using the formal address to be informal. 'You're getting more impatient with every passing year. Since when did a crew ever start assembling before ten o'clock? And even if they did, you'd be grumbling because they were kicking their heels waiting for the dew to lift on the spreading ground. Why don't you take the pail and go off for the beer?'

'The bar doesn't open till eleven o'clock, that's why. And it's not going to take me an hour to walk to the bar, bad and all as my feet are!'

'There's nothing wrong with your feet since Dr MacBeth fixed them. And in any case it's not your feet that will delay you but your tongue by the time you meet a score of people that you haven't met in a month. And there'll be plenty of those around, this being, as you say, Saturday.'

'They'll be a change from a female tongue anyway!' He winked at me as he picked up the enamelled pail and set off. Their badinage was unusual, but it was in keeping with the mood of the miniscular carnival which was the peat-crewing day; and the beer pail was part of the ritual. There was no reason why it should be; the word 'screw-top' had long since been absorbed into the vernacular and the Sabbath roadside tended to glint with the occasional empty bottle from Saturday night's 'carry-out'; but the middle-aged men of the peat-crewing would have regarded 'screw-tops' as boozing, or infra dig like corned beef for Sunday dinner, whereas a middle of the day mug from the pail of flat beer followed by a satisfied sigh and a rasp of the back of the hand across the chin was as much part of the tradition of peat day as was the custom that the man of the house cut only the first peat of the day from his own bank, and, for the rest of the time played host.

'Well, men, that was a good day's work well done,' said Big Grandfather after he put the amen to the grace after the long and sumptuous meal served up by Grannie and the helping village wives at the end of the day. 'I'm glad it's Sunday tomorrow and that I have a full day before I have to start repaying.' The fact that grandfather was making a little joke was

154

proof that he was highly pleased with his crew's efforts.

'Fine for you,' said somebody of his own age. 'You got the Saturday cut and your peat will get their first day's drying while you're at your prayers. See and don't be studying their progress on your way to and from church!'

The conversation pursued its leisurely aimless course as the pipes were lit and the women got on with washing the dishes. It was Alasdair Norman from the Kyles Skerries crofts who, as usual, introduced a note of pessimism into the easy-osiness of the chat.

'Well, it's been getting harder and harder to get peat-crews together for the last year or two, but I doubt if we'll get one at all next year if what I hear is true –'

'What on earth are you talking about?'

'Do you remember that strange fellow who turned up by accident at the Moderator's day in Scarista?'

'What of him?' somebody asked while one or two chuckled as they remembered Geordie MacLellan's discomfiture.

'They're saying he was some kind of a spy from the Government, checking on the possibility of raising the militia again, and –'

'The Territorial Army,' said my second cousin Archie who with his twin brother Neil the Banker were the youngest members of the peat-crew. 'Somebody was telling Neil that there's been an army general going round the southern islands making a count of the young men who might be willing to volunteer. Just making a count.'

'Well I hope neither of you is fool enough to volunteer!' Neil and Archie glanced at each other but said nothing; they were so close that people used to say of them that they could carry on a conversation with each other without talking.

'War, war, war,' said my grandfather. 'If it comes to that it'll be the third one in my memory, but I pray that men will come to their senses. If it comes to war it'll be men who fought in the last one who'll start it, and that's just beyond belief.'

A few weeks later, Captain Derek Lang and Viscount Fincastle arrived in Harris to call for recruits for the 4th Battalion (the Territorial Battalion) of the Queen's Own Cameron Highlanders, and in one night eighty-nine young men from the small island of Harris volunteered. Archie and

Neil were among the first. Within a couple of weeks their numbers had grown to about a hundred. It had been a stroke of brilliant public relations to make Lord Fincastle Company Commander. His grandparents, Lord and Lady Dunmore, had been proprietors of the whole of Harris at the end of the last century. He had been a sympathetic and progressive landlord; she had seen the potential of local tweed and had established the Harris Tweed Industry, which was to become the foundation of the economy of the island, and despite its susceptibility to world market fluctuations had remained so for generations. The Dunmores had not only done much to counter the bitterness which their predecessors had engendered in Harris with policies of exploitation, repression and, frequently, eviction, but they had set a precedent for good landlordship for their successors and we were, as a result, reasonably free of the antipathy which sours relationships between landlords and crofters in other parts of the West Highlands. While the vast majority of our men would have spat at the idea of 'touching their bonnets to the laird' there lingered on two traditions which met when Captain Lang did his recruitment drive – the age-old instinct in the Highlander to respond to 'the call to arms' despite the disaster that that response had sometimes brought to his country and his race, and the equally aged instinct to look to the laird for the leadership as he would, once upon a time, have looked to his Clan Chief. Now, less than half a century on, that whole exposition may sound ridiculous; but it wasn't then. And it wasn't only 'Dubby' Fincastle that Captain Lang was fortunate in; the landlord of our new village was a peppery ex-Colonel who commanded a great deal of respect and his son Gavin (well-liked and handsome and, as events were to prove, heroic) became one of Lang's first officers. So the Harrismen were led from the beginning by men whose pedigrees they knew; and the non-commissioned infrastructure was local too – the popular 'Bunt' Macdonald of the local Bank of Scotland became Colour Sergeant and his colleague, my second cousin Neil, became Corporal. They even had one of the best pipers of the Hebrides in Peter Roses.

Of course the whole thing was a game. There was going to be no war. And the initial parades and exercises were a welcome diversion in a place where regular entertainment tended to begin and end with the Saturday promenade. When rifles and a Lewis Gun and hand-grenades began to arrive they only added piquancy to the ploy, and even the old women used to take their knitting out to the hillocks on lovely summer evenings and watch the lads shooting at targets and causing bangs and mini mushroom clouds of peat when they practised throwing their grenades into peat pools. When the uniforms arrived the whole thing took on a new theatricality; the populace of Tarbert would turn out to watch the Company march down the street with Peter Ross at their head with the bagpipe. Even the soldiers themselves weren't yet taking it all seriously; some of the dedicated ones would march with their eyes determinedly forward; a few of the more self-conscious would stumble and blush crimson to their bonnets when they heard a 'look at our Sandy' from a doting aunt or grannie; occasionally a cock-sure braggart would wink suggestively in the direction of a buxom area of the crowd without breaking step or concentration.

There was a time when these youths had been our idols and sometimes our friends. On Sunday afternoon walks we would be allowed to consort with them and scrounge cigarettes from them; in their own homes they would treat us as equals; up till now it was only on the Saturday promenade that they spurned us as we hung around on the edge of their courtings like pups vainly hoping for a nibble of the big dogs' bones. The uniforms and the rifles moved them out of our ken all together; even the third year girls who, hitherto, might have held out an occasional grape of Tantallus in our direction, now looked down their noses at us and, on manoeuvre evenings in particular, walked round the village with their gym-frock belts tightened to strangulation and looking stuck-up and stuck-out. It was galling, but, far from resenting the 'Terriers' as they had come to be called, it inflamed our chauvinism; we all wanted to be soldiers and get into uniform; we would have falsified our ages if that had been legally possible or physically credible. A few of the Tarbert boys were members of the local Boy Scout troop, and we country yokels had hitherto regarded them as nancy-boys. But suddenly their khaki hats and tunics and neckerchiefs represented a uniform. I rushed to the scoutmaster and enlisted – three days before he decided that his duties with the Territorials were taking up all his spare time,

157

and, in the absence of anybody able and willing to take over from him, the troop was disbanded. I must be the shortest serving Boy Scout on record.

While the 'uniform fever' (it was by no stretch of the imagination war fever) gripped a large portion of the community, there was one section which reacted totally differently. The older men, those who had served in the 1914-18 war, with very few exceptions withdrew into a silence. They would occasionally turn out to watch an official march past or parade, but they watched it with none of the fun-of-the-fair attitude of the rest. When somebody occasionally committed a gaffe – and there were occasional ones since commands spat out in English did not always get a crisp accurate response from recruits who thought in Gaelic – the older men would smile with smiles that rarely reached their eyes. There was a subtle change in their social pattern too; they took to going to town two or three evenings a week and the traditional rendezvous in the cobbler's shop was abandoned. Instead they took to meeting in the watchmaker's shop where there was a modern efficient wireless set, and they would stand around and discuss and dissect the evening news bulletin before returning slowly back home. Such optimism as they clung to dissolved as they heard of the German-Russian Pact and the Dutch call-up; it vanished completely when the British Navy was mobilised. On Saturday 2nd September the whole community knew that the make-believe was over when the Territorials got telegrams telling them to prepare to embark on the cargo boat *Clydesdale* on Monday.

Nobody heard Chamberlain's formal declaration of war on the Sunday because, in the Hebrides in those days, radio sets were never switched on on Sunday – not even for the news. But they didn't need to hear.

Long before the normal hour of worship people were streaming along the three roads, some heading for the Free Presbyterian Church on the edge of the town; some for the Church of Scotland down at the shore. There wasn't an empty seat in either. The normal observation of family pews went by the board although, of course, families still crowded together even more than usual. Like the rest, Grandfather's pew had strangers in it and I, along with the other young folk, was ushered into the standing area below the gallery. Although the church was fuller than I had ever seen it even at communion time there was an atmosphere of hush, and the huge congregation even seemed to move in silence when they stood up for the prayers. It was only when the minister began to pray specifically for the boys who were going away 'to fight a just war' that there was a little noise from here and there as, here and there, a woman sobbed against her will ...

The *Clydesdale* didn't arrive on Monday. Word came that she was threading her way up through the southern isles – Barra, South Uist, Benbecula and North Uist, picking up the Territorials from there. But, on Tuesday afternoon, Tarbert pier was packed with people from every airt of Harris. The Territorials had marched crisply the short distance from the Drill Hall to the pier with Piper Ross playing ahead of them, but now they had been stood down and each soldier, with his pack on his back and trailing his rifle, was standing surrounded by his family and relatives; here and there a girl friend had abandoned the secrecy of courtship and, probably for the first time, joined the boy's parents. The *Clydesdale* seemed to take an age from the time that she appeared behind the Minister's Islands at the mouth of the bay and the old tub, scheduled for retirement, was lower in the water than she had been for many a day. As she crept closer the sound of bagpipes came on ahead of her, long before one could hear the thud of her engines. 'The Uist boys' somebody said with a smile and, somehow or other, that eased the tension and the conversation spread out of its private knots. The Uistmen were, and are, superb pipers and ready to tune in to joy or sorrow. There were a lot of them playing but they fell silent as the ship tied up and scores of soldiers in their spick and span uniforms crowded the rails to cheer the Harris contingent as it marched, single file, up the gangway. In minutes the gangway was being lifted again and the Clydesdale's engines thudded astern. She began to creep carefully away from the jetty where there was now complete silence, but as the last hawser was thrown clear a solitary male voice began to precent a psalm in the traditional Gaelic way and from shore and ship voices welled up to chant the lines after him,

> 'God is our refuge and our strength
> In straits a present aid ...'

Chapter Twelve

Laughter was slow to return; but it did. Just as bereavement, no matter how intense or how personal, has to surrender its sorrowful indulgence to the pressures of ordinary living, so a community has to adjust itself even to the sudden creaming off of its most vibrant members. And there was no immediate tragedy to turn an international war into a family's war. The Territorials who left Tarbert pier on the *Clydesdale* had teamed up with a further contingent from Skye and had joined up in Inverness with other elements of the famous 51st Highland Division – the Seaforths, the Gordons, the Argylls and the Black Watch. That much we knew, despite the immediate censorship clamp-down, because most of the families of the Northlands had relatives in Inverness and their communications were not subject to scrutiny like the mail from the soldiers themselves. So, while the lads in Dochfour camp were desperately trying to invent codes to communicate what they were up to, the people at home knew their every movement through the good offices of the Invernessians. The West Highlands and the Western Isles were immediately declared a 'protected area' because of the number of naval establishments there and because the north of Scotland was fast becoming a rendezvous area for the Atlantic convoys. People needed 'passport' certificates to move out of the area, or more especially come into it, and that for a while became an irritation and gave a feeling that we were in mild state of seige. The Territorials came home for Christmas leave, not having been farther afield than Aldershot, and their very presence, first footing in their uniforms, and looking fit and cheerful, created a vague sort of feeling that our worries had been exaggerated and that nothing serious was going to befall them after all. Since periods and epochs aren't designated till afterwards we weren't to know that what we were going through was later to become known as 'the phoney war'.

Not that we were under any illusions about the reality of it for other people. We were hearing more and more about air raids on the southern cities; news like the fall of Warsaw (although it was only an unknown town in a far away country) warned us that the Germans were not being halted as easily as we fondly imagined they would be. The stunning news that the *Royal Oak* was sunk in Scapa Flow with a loss of 800 lives (the equivalent of a third of our total island population as someone put it) created an awesome fear in an island where the majority of families had somebody facing the war at sea; the vast majority of our serving men were, in fact, in the Merchant Service or in the Royal Navy; the war was crystallised for us round the army only because we had seen, with our own eyes, the departure of one hundred men in one compact unit. And for me, personally, that crystallisation was inevitable because Archie and Neil whom I hero worshipped were part of that unit. Grandfather and Grandmother had a much more personal interest which caused them more anxiety than they ever revealed; not only was their son (my uncle) at sea, but his wife and baby son were in Southampton and very much in the firing line as the air raids began to intensify.

Everywhere the word *news* was acquiring a new urgency and significance. 'What's the news?' no longer meant 'What's fresh in your part of the world?'; it meant 'What is the very latest that you have heard about the war?' It had taken us a long time to get used to the immediacy of the daily newspaper stories; as the war had been seen to be approaching the radio had speeded up information and made people feel that they should be abreast with the day; that same radio was now urging us into thinking of the world changing hour by hour. Radio was still a relative novelty and by no means every house had a set; Grandfather didn't, and my own parents back in the Southlands didn't. At first most people had thought it was a luxury they could afford to do

161

without, and by the time they began to regard it as a necessity radio sets had become very hard to get because the nation's manufacturing resources were being channelled into the war effort. One was fortunate if one could buy a second hand set, and that remained the case till the pressures of public demand resulted in the famous 'utility sets' in their spartan white-wood as opposed to the sedate and luxurious walnuts and mahoganies and oaks of their forerunners.

In Tarbert the cobbler's shop had never recovered its place as the village council chamber; although the little old cobbler still crouched over his last by lamplight into the late hours of the night few of his former cronies now congregated around him and he began to look lonelier and lonelier. But the watchmaker's shop had boomed; one had to be early in the queue if one were to get reasonably near the loudspeaker (and one needed to be close because the quality of reception still left a lot to be desired) and when the black-out started one almost had to book a seat. It was only on a Friday or a Saturday night that I could hope to get to the watchmaker's anyway, because The Blus kept up his patrol in war as assiduously as he had done in the peace. When I did so I tried to store up every scrap of information that I heard so that I could relay the latest news to my grandparents when I got home.

Grandfather had given up going to town at night, and because most of the young men were away, he saw few visitors. His only regular link to the sources of immediate news was Ali who, if he had ever contemplated a return to his native land, was now firmly cut off from any such escape; as if a wife and family were not enough to anchor him he now had the whole naval resources of Nazi Germany between him and the vast homeland which was still just India in the British Raj. The one way in which Ali had not been able to take a full role in the crofting community was that he didn't have a cow. He had a few sheep which he was allowed to graze on the hill pastures and which some crofter or other would tend for him during lambing time. But, living in rented accommodation in Tarbert, it was not very practical for him to keep a cow. So, night after night, except Sunday, he trudged out to Big Grandfather's to buy milk – oblivious to winter gales or lightning or thunder. As soon as he had heard the nine o'clock news Ali set off for Grandfather's, occasionally giving a

162

lonely traveller the fright of his life when he smiled at him suddenly out of the dark, and, having arrived, he would plonk himself on the nearest chair and launch into a recitation of the nine o'clock bulletin. The only occasional preface he put to his monologue was, 'Tonight the news was told by Joseph MacLeod' as if the fact that he had the same surname as grandfather gave that distinguished newsreader's message an added validity. I was, by then, tolerably fluent in English but I had to strain my ears and my knowledge and my imagination to make some sense out of Ali's fractured rendering of the news. Grandfather, who spoke good English but whose ear wasn't attuned to the standard versions far less Ali's must have ended up with some rather bizarre impressions of the progress of the conflict, particularly when Lord Haw-Haw started broadcasting his propaganda bulletins, which Ali listened to and always edited into his recollections of the BBC version. Occasionally, when matters appeared to be getting out of hand, I would sit with a mournful Grandfather after Ali had left and try to explain to him that half the Royal Navy had not been sunk in Coventry, and could not possibly have been since Coventry was reasonably remote from the seas. That was when Ali had got some of Haw-Haw's more extravagant claims mixed up with the BBC's account of a bombing raid, or else Grandfather had failed to follow Ali's bad grammar and exotic accent.

The passing on of news by word of mouth through second and third parties is a hazardous business at the best of times, but doubly so when it is being sifted through two thought processes (one operating in Hindu and the other in Gaelic) before being reconstituted in broken English. Even back home in the Southlands the problems applied although not in the same way. Because our village had been founded by veterans from the First World War, our men were too old and their sons too young, by and large, for either generation to be called on to participate actively in the second one. But nobody can be totally exempt from war. And though our little village contributed only two or three people to the services there were relatives by the score in the army and even more in the merchant marine. For that reason news of every action was awaited anxiously, and because the first war was still fresh in the minds of the men who had survived it, the walls of every house were covered with the war maps

163

which were being copiously supplied by various newspapers, and the movements of navies and armies were plotted with little pins as if Scaristavore were at the nerve centre of command. News was in demand, therefore, at two levels – at the professional level, by those who still had a lingering interest in the tactical disposition of military forces, and emotionally by those who had relatives or friends 'away'. In the Southlands wirelesses were in even shorter supply than they were among the more sophisticated citizenry of Tarbert. Calum the Post was getting old, but, just as he had always been our principal contact with the outside world, there now devolved on him the duty of chief war correspondent by virtue of the fact that he had the best radio set in the parish. He was more accurate than Ali with his reportage but much more temperamental, and if the mood took him he might, out of sheer cussedness, refuse to stop at a house unless he had a letter to deliver. 'I am paid to deliver news with a stamp on it' was his defence if anybody chided him for being neglectful.

Because there was no electricity in Harris then (outside establishments with their own private generators) all the wirelesses were powered by a large 'dry' battery which had a long and fairly predictable life, and by a 'wet' battery known as an accumulator which had to be taken to some generating centre, like the nearest wool mill, to be re-charged when it became exhausted. Accumulators were exasperating things. There was no way of anticipating their demise because the duration of each charge depended on the conscientiousness of the electrician administering it, and, of course, on the length of the period during which the radio set was in use. In a house where the younger members of the family had predilections for Scottish dance music, the sudden demise of the accumulator tended to have the sort of explosive effect that the telephone bill has nowadays on a house with daughters.

'What's the news today, Calum?' enquired a devout old lady who had a finely honed relish for grief.

It was the umpteenth time that Calum had been asked the same question that morning, and his patience wasn't elastic at the best of times.

'The accumulator's down!' he shouted, crashing his red van into gear so that he didn't hear the old lady's anguished moan of,

'God help us! I wonder how many island boys lost their lives on that one.' Since most things travelled faster than Calum, bad news certainly did, and, by the time he reached the ninth house on, having been overtaken by a couple of bicycles, the information was awaiting him that a large merchant ship had been sunk and scores of Hebridean seamen had been lost. Which news, for lack of any other, Calum passed on to the rest of the houses on his route. It took him a while to unravel why, two or three days later, he found himself being accused of the new crime of the age – 'spreading alarm and despondency', and why few people were inclined to believe him when he did pass on a piece of 'highly confidential information' to the effect that, in response to a personal appeal from the Government, Colonel Walker, the landlord, was going to mobilise the entire male population of the Southlands and form them into an armed defence regiment to be known as the LDV.

'Rubbish!' said most people.

'Why not?' wondered my father. 'If the Government thinks us important enough to give us our own wee Lysander to protect us, it's not beyond the bounds of possibility that they would think of sticking guns into our hands to protect ourselves. They don't know some of the people in this place!' The 'wee Lysander' to which he referred was a little spotter plane which was on permanent patrol in our area and as the U-boat attacks on merchant shipping became more menacing the sound of the Lysander became as familiar as the croak of the corncrake and its appearances much more common. As the menace of the war became more oppressive after the shattering news of Dunkirk, aircraft activity above the sea-lanes became more and more intense. Occasionally one would hear the tell-tale stop-start drone of an enemy plane and under those circumstances the homely chug of 'our own wee Lysander' was a comfort; a symbol of the impregnable ring of defence which we imagined to be surrounding us.

In the Northlands, I was only vaguely aware of the activities in the village, and such information as I did get was only sketchily conveyed by my mother in her letters, which still reached me regularly on Tuesdays. Her news tended to concentrate more on domestic issues – the nuisance of local merchants insisting on sticking rigidly to the 'points' allocated in the ration books, the

165

record number of socks that a certain local woman had contributed to some area of the war effort; the fact that father was getting a new loom now that there was a dramatic upsurge in the sale of Harris Tweed. The news that tended to interest me most were the items introduced 'Your father says to tell you ...' and it was under that heading that I heard about Calum and the accumulator, the rumours about the arming of the village, and the sad news that the Golf Course was being closed down ... The distance between myself and the village was steadily getting greater although the miles remained the same. I was by way of becoming more and more a boy of the Northlands (whence, after all, I had originally come) and the pressures of schoolwork, which happily was now beginning to prove more congenial as I devoted more time to it, were adding to the distancing. The highlights and the tragedies of 'my war' were the ones which most deeply affected the Northlands and, consequently, most immediately, the young soldiers who had sailed from Tarbert Pier six months before. We knew they were now in France – in the Saar. We knew that because Archie had been home on leave.

Dunkirk came as numbing news. It was impossible to believe that the great British army was in retreat; Britain just didn't lose wars, according to the history books. But there it was, being relayed day by day for a whole week from the watchmaker's radio to the knot of people that now never seemed to leave the shop door. One could sense a slow depression spreading through the community; it wasn't that people discussed the business so much as the fact that they didn't smile so much any more. Even in school much of the laughter had gone out of the boys who still congregated in the lavatory for the morning and afternoon interval smokes, and the conversation wasn't any more the chit-chat of local happenings or the prurience of sexual fantasising. The incredible achievement of the evacuation didn't, for a long time, penetrate; the BBC might pump out heroic stories about rowing boats and pleasure yachts snatching men off the beaches under fire; the news might hint optimistically about the day when the British army would return. But, as far as we were concerned, the blunt truth was that a powerful army of 400,000 men had been defeated. There was one pathetic glimmer of hope. The 51st Division was still in France. The

Highlanders had not retreated. And were they not, after all, the kilted warriors that the Germans had dreaded most in that other war as 'the ladies from Hell?' When they fixed bayonets ... when the pipers began to play ... when ... when ... when ...

It was a braggart euphoria, and the dispelling of it was doubly agonising because it was so slow. A week after Dunkirk had passed into the legend the news came that the 51st Highland Division had been captured at St Valery en Caux where all attempts at a Dunkirk type evacuation had been frustrated. This was reality. This was no longer a case of an army being routed or captured; these were our own kith and kin – the lads who had sailed on the Clydesdale from Tarbert. The agony was so much the worse because it contained a glimmer of hope; after all the dreaded telegram that told of death put an end to hope, but if a man was taken prisoner of war there was the knowledge that he would return home one day. The surrender hadn't happened without casualties – we knew that from the few telegrams that did come; the dreadful business was not knowing and the waiting, from day to day, till a list of prisoners would be announced. For many it was a long, long wait, and my own people were among those most desperately on the rack. There had been no news of Archie since he had gone back to France after that last leave of his, and nobody knew whether he and Neil were prisoners, or wounded, or dead. Rumours sprang out of the empty air, and they only served to make the waiting worse.

But, from St Valery on, the mood changed; the dull resignation gave way to bitterness and the war was no longer the war against Germany; as Hitler ranted about the total annihilation of the enemies of the Reich it became 'Hitler's war'. He, personally, it was who had been responsible for the loss of our hundred men – whether by imprisonment or death. The British propaganda machine was swinging effectively into action too and, as the threatened invasion didn't immediately materialise, the sense of sorrow gave way to a sense of defiance save in the individual grieving breast. 'Call-up' was yet another word that became absorbed into the Gaelic vocabulary and, week after week, an individual or a couple of individuals would board the mailboat in Sunday best and carrying a small suitcase; but never again was there to be a mass departure with pomp and ceremony such as there had been with the Terriers.

In school, some of the boys were now beginning to talk about the day when they would enlist. After all some of them were approaching sixteen and soon would be liable for conscription anyway; most of these would have volunteered there and then if they were allowed to, but there was no way that parents would tolerate a falsification of ages. Those parents who hadn't experienced the grimness of the battle-front in the first war, had experienced the traumas of bereavement or waiting and wondering in the second.

Bit by bit the Saturday night parade was re-establishing itself although there was now a marked accent on school pupils, but it was reviving because there was nothing better to do. The excitement had gone out of it except on the rare occasion when a small group of sailors happened to be home on leave, or when a naval vessel put into East Loch Tarbert and a swaggering group of ratings with strange accents came ashore in search of the kind of fun which, by and large, vanished behind closed doors as soon as fathers heard the chugging of the pinnaces. Whatever hopes the sailors clutched as they tied up at the pier soon vanished and they were left with only an all-male bar in which liquor supplies were running low, and a gaggle of scruffy schoolboys trying to scrounge cigarettes from them.

Yet another reason that the parade was losing its excitement was that the heart was going out of the shops as anything resembling luxury merchandise disappeared from the shelves. There was no longer any point in remaining open late on a Saturday night. Ali was doubly hit. His main customers for his vanity goods had sailed on the *Clydesdale* and although his window still shimmered with toiletry there was no profit to be made out of school children crushing their noses up against his window; worse still the increasingly strict black-out regulations meant that the glitter was killed stone dead when the blinds were dropped. At last he announced that he was going to close down and he approached a member of my school class to ask if he could muster a team of six strong lads for the following Saturday night to move his stock out of the shop into store. Poor innocent Ali!

When we descended on the shop at eight o'clock he had all his goods carefully packed into large cardboard cartons which, in his innocence, he didn't even bother to seal. There began a

168

shuttle service of carriers from the little shop down to the store at the end of his house where his wife was waiting to take delivery of the boxes, and to check that the number of cartons that left the shop reached the store. What neither of them realised was that on the way down, half-way between the shop and the store and out of sight of both, there was an empty garage into which we had long-since forced entry so that we could use it as a smoking hide-away out of the ken of 'The Blus'. Every promising carton was carried into the garage and hastily ransacked for the luxuries that we had coveted in the shop window for months. Bottles of brilliantine, jars of hair-cream, scented soaps, after-shave lotion ... everything that savoured of unattainable luxury was there. We pillaged ruthlessly but discreetly. We left the cigarettes alone because we knew that Ali was bound to have count of them; we were tempted by the condoms but should they ever be discovered in our possession we'd be in dire trouble; deep down we knew that the chances of our using them were slim indeed and when one of our number declared that a friend of his had said that their usage was 'like having a bath in an oilskin' that was a good enough face-saving formula. By the time we were finished there was a discreet hoard of toiletries hidden under a scrap of tarpaulin in a dark corner of the garage; the spoils ranged from solidified brilliantine to rather sophisticated eau-de-Cologne. At the end of the night we had the ill grace to accept twenty cigarettes and a shilling each from Ali before slipping back under cover of dark to the garage to divide the spoils. In all fairness we took only sufficient for our own long term needs and a little over to share with our friends.

Half-way down the path to my grandfather's house I met the old man on his way to look for me. I prayed that the Sabbath hadn't arrived. It hadn't, but it didn't make any difference; all the way down to the house I got a tongue lashing such as I had never suspected him to be capable of, but it was nothing compared to what Grannie had to say as I snuffled my way through supper careful not to jerk as I moved lest the tins and the bottles in my pockets rattled. I had meant to conceal my hoard among the hay in the byre on my way home but, by meeting me, Big Grandfather had foiled that. I had to sweat my way through Saturday night prayers, moving like a cripple lest I clank when it came to kneeling for the final prayer. I was what I imagined a nervous wreck must be by the time I got upstairs and got my loot concealed behind the most innocent looking books in my make-shift book-case. I left a tin of solid brilliantine beside the mirror on my dressing table, fairly certain that neither Grandmother nor Grandfather would assume that it was other than purchased out of my pocket money.

By Sunday morning the lateness of my home-coming was either forgotten or forgiven and Grandfather was mildly complimentary about the alacrity with which I had sprung out of bed as soon as I heard him shuffling downstairs. He even complimented me on my appearance as I sat at breakfast with my hair flattened under a weight of brilliantine; if he smelt the toilet water with which I had laved myself he made no comment. As we set off together for church, up the path on which he had met me in wrath twelve hours before, our normal relationship had been totally restored. It was a morning of glorious sunshine with a twittering harmony of birds, and, as we walked along chatting to friends and neighbours making their ways to worship, my conscience didn't trouble me a whit. It was like one of the Sundays of the year before except that the church bell was silent.

Church was crowded as it had been every Sabbath since the day the war began. The absence of the young men in the services was made up for many times over by parents and grandparents and relatives who came to offer up their prayers of supplication and of thanks. The boats from Scalpay, Drinishadder and Scadabay had tied up at the pier as we approached the church and their passengers had joined the leisurely column making its way up the path past Ali's house or else made their ways to the Free Presbyterian Church up the hill.

I had always associated the shore kirk with cool and camphor, but only the latter was in evidence that day as I sat hunched tightly between my grandfather and my stoutest aunt. The sun, beating through the kirk windows, appeared to have singled out our pew and the one in front in which sat two of my fellow looters from the night before. I noted that their hair was plastered flat like my own and both heads were gleaming like the flanks of well groomed horses. I knew that the other three were somewhere in the church, but I couldn't remember which were their landladies' pews and even if I had done I could no more swivel round to look for them than a sheaf of corn could have stood on end in an autumn stack. I was already trying a rhythm whereby I could breathe in when my aunt was breathing out. Apart from my partners in crime in front of me I was aware of only two faces at the end of their respective pews; one was The Blus whose jaw was twitching as he discreetly sucked at a peppermint; the other was Ali who was staring straight ahead of him with the impassivity of his race. The war had apparently converted him. At last the minister appeared through the door that opened into his pulpit, high above the one in which the precentor had long since taken his seat with much sighing and massaging of his eyes. The minister announced the first psalm and after the precentor had stood up and coughed discreetly a couple of times he led the congregation into a mighty volume of singing. He was, of course, the only one standing; I would have to await that relief till the first prayer. My aunt was a mighty singer and although my grandfather enunciated a note here and there he went through the whole chest expansion process as if he were tackling a Wagnerian aria; between them I felt like a baby mouse trapped in the bellows of an accordion. But my troubles were only beginning.

By the end of the first verse my Harris Tweed suit was beginning to pull at my body hairs as the lustiness of the singing seemed to generate heat additional to that of the beating sun. The second verse was half way through when I became aware of a rivulet of what I assumed to be sweat oozing down my temple and I realised to my horror that I didn't have a handkerchief. With my elbow wedged tightly between my aunt and myself I managed to get the tips of my fingers to my forehead before the perspiration reached my eye, but as soon as I felt the oily slitheriness I realised what was happening. My solid brilliantine was melting in the heat of the kirk; and I knew that there was nothing that I could do to stop it melting. My grandfather elbowed me sharply to stop me wriggling, and all I could do was look helplessly at my two friends in front to see how they were faring. Not much better. Except that they had handkerchiefs with which they could mop themselves discreetly from time to time, while I could only sit still and allow the oily rivulets to follow the contours of my face down into the collar of my shirt; I prayed God that the word VIOLET on the tin on my dressing-table referred to the scent and not the colour.

My aunt sniffed after she had lashed out at the last note of that interminable psalm. The minister sniffed and looked around the church before he called us to prayer, probably wondering if he had strayed into a chapel by some ghastly mistake. Somebody sniffed at the far end of the church during the prayer, and by the time the minister got round to his first reading the church sounded like an ill-mannered kindergarten smitten by flu. One fragile old lady left hastily clutching her handkerchief to her mouth, and one of the elders hurried out after her. The benediction brought to an end the longest church service I have ever known. Strangely enough the only person to make any comment was a navyman from Scalpay who turned to his companion as he got out of the door of the church and said, 'What the hell was going on in church today; the place smelt like a Hong Kong whorehouse!' Heads whipped round to look at him in disbelief and he fell silent.

It was the last Sunday of term, and on the Monday, after school, I smuggled my hoard out of the house and hid it in an unlikely corner of the byre where there was little chance of my grandfather discovering it. I could risk taking only one bottle of hair-dressing home with me without attracting questions and, worse still, giving the impression that I had pocket money to spare.

My arrival home for the long summer break was a happier one by far than that dreaded Christmas one which now seemed a life-time away. I had in my pocket the first report card which I had received since that disastrous preliminary one, and it showed a dramatic improvement – particularly in English, which I knew would please my father most. This was my fourth visit back home, including one long mid-term week-end, and nobody came to meet the bus any more with any special welcome. This time such shocks as were in store were for me. In what had hitherto been the front porch there stood a compact little iron loom with two pedals instead of four; I knew it to be the new Hattersley loom, popularly known as 'the automatic' to which many Hebridean weavers had finally been converted and which was already beginning to revolutionise the Harris Tweed industry. But there was a greater shock in store when I opened the door into the living room. My father was sitting at the end of the table filling in some official looking forms; he was in an ill-fitting khaki uniform, and behind him, propped up against the wall, was a rifle.

172

Chapter Thirteen

Nobody ever had 'a good war' and I can't imagine how anybody could coin the phrase in cynicism or in jest. But because, on the Atlantic coast of the Hebrides, we were about as remote from the 'action' as it was possible to be, we didn't suffer the horrors experienced, as time went on, by people living in Liverpool or London or Glasgow. Nor did we suffer the privations of day to day living to the same extent. Just as the sea and the land had saved us during the Depression years, so the natural resources of the countryside spared us from the stringency of rationing, and, by and large, we depended on the little buff ration books only for things which would have been considered luxuries in our part of the world two or three generations back. We had our own hens, our own eggs, milk, potatoes and fish; and every crofter had his own flock of sheep. There were stringent laws governing the butchering of sheep and cattle, but London laws were hard to enforce in the Western isles at the best of times and doubly hard when communications were doubly worse! No law could be invented that would prevent a wedder or a crock disappearing in a quagmire or falling over a cliff, and while Lord Woolton at the Ministry of Food was gaining plaudits for spreading resources so that the nation as a whole was reasonably nourished, there was little he could do to stop parts of it being better nourished than others. George Morrison, the celebrated humorist of the *Stornoway Gazette* defined the Government's dilemma in a poem which caused much hilarity at the time.

173

There's no wether on the tether
Where the wether used to be;
But there's meat upon the rafter
Which Lord Woolton must not see.
They say it was the weather
Which the wether couldn't stand –
That it died of influenza …
But the smell of it is grand.

We were deeply conscious of the shortages from which our
cousins in the cities suffered and we tried to help. It was perhaps
fortunate that Government officials were otherwise busily
engaged and didn't have time to wonder at the steady stream of
large parcels labelled 'Books with care' that left the islands by
every mailboat as we sought to share our bounty of fresh mutton
and poultry and black puddings with our less fortunate relations.
But the smell of the roast coming from the oven that day was
somehow unfamiliar.

'Good Lord, boy,' said my father. 'What are you doing here?
The bus isn't due for an hour yet.'

I explained to him that the bus service had been cut from twice
daily to thrice weekly to save petrol and this was its new schedule
time.

'Nobody ever tells us anything. Your mother will be mortified
that she's not home to meet you, and her with a nice haunch of
venison roasting for your home-coming. I hear that you deserve
more than the prodigal son's mere calf this time.' I had written
to my mother telling her of the improvement in my marks and I
could see that my lapse of the winter term had been forgiven.

'Where did the venison come from?'

'Och I've always said that Colonel Walker was a good
landlord. I hear that some of the LDV boys on the mainland are
going around with khaki bands on their arms and practising
with hay-forks and pikes and things, but when Churchill heard
that we had a ready-made full Colonel to lead us he ordered
nine Welsh Guardsmen to be stripped of their uniforms and
rifles so that they could be sent to us. "We must hold Harris," he
said in the House of Commons …' My father smiled ruefully as
he looked down at his midriff. 'Mind you, it must have been a
devil of a big Welsh Guardsman who had this uniform; I could

174

take another fellow inside it with me.' I didn't care about the uniform. I couldn't take my eyes off the rifle. I couldn't take in the idea of my father with a rifle. Over the years he would never tolerate a gun in the house although I had pleaded, over and over again, to be allowed to borrow a neighbour's shot-gun to shoot rabits. Whatever he had gone through, during his four years as a sniper in the first war, had turned him bitterly against guns forever.

'Can I fire it some time?'

The question had come out automatically, and even when he heaved himself to his feet I couldn't believe that he was going to agree.

'Why not? Just once, seeing you did so well in your test in school, and seeing your mother isn't here to meet you. And besides I know that you'll never stop pestering me till I agree.' I stared in fascination as he pulled back the bolt and fed in two shells. 'One shot, mind you. And I'll probably get court-martialled!'

He stopped as we were going through the porch, which had now been converted into a weaving shed for the new Hattersley.

'You were quick enough to spot the rifle but you didn't say anything about the new loom. But I'll tell you something. This one shot is going to cost you ten yards of tweed woven on that loom as soon as I get a few minutes to show you how to use it. It'll be fun for you. It's just like pedalling a bicycle.' I'd have agreed to weave ten tweeds, far less ten yards.'

There were several round iron lids from sheep-dip pails lying out at the end of the house. He picked one up and, with a lump of the red keel that we used for marking sheep, he drew concentric rings on it till it began to look like a reasonable imitation of a target.

'Go and stand that up against the old mid-way dyke!'

'The mid-way dyke? Will it fire that far? That's four hundred yards!'

'A 303 bullet will travel a mile, even if not accurately. That's why you've always got to have your target up against a sand-bag or a hill or something. On you go!'

I went off like the wind and placed the target where he had instructed me; by the time I got back to him he was on his stomach resting on his elbows and nestling the butt against his cheek.

'I'm warning you, you've got to hold the butt really tightly against your shoulder or she'll break your collar-bone when she kicks. The idea is to get the bead at the end of the barrel into the V of the back-sight; you start with your gun pointing at the bottom of the target and then you lift the barrel up gently till the V and the bead and the bulls-eye are in one line. Do you understand?' Before I could reply he had fired, completely casually, or so it seemed, and a hole appeared in the middle of the little spot which was the bulls-eye.

His eyes were strangely icy as he handed me the gun.

'One shot,' he snapped as he levered the bolt and cleared the breech.

I got down and aimed for all I was worth and ended up with a bruised shoulder and a target unscathed.

'See what I told you? Man, that bullet of yours is still travelling; it'll probably end up in the Minch.'

When he got inside he dropped the lead of the pull-through into the breech end of the barrel and got me to heave it through. When he was satisfied that it was as clean as new he put the rifle into the loft. I never saw him fire the gun again although he went off with it twice a week to drill. One of his fellow Home Guardsmen (as they came to be called) told me afterwards that, at rifle practice, father merely jerked the gun as the others fired but never pulled the trigger himself. Later, he slipped his unused bullets to whoever was due to go and investigate the deer forest next, on condition that he got the shell casings back so that he could claim his next allocation of bullets. Apparently Colonel Walker could never understand why a man who had been a soldier in the first war couldn't even hit the target. Poor Colonel Walker. It must have been a sore trial to him to be ordered by the Government to issue his tenants with a rifle and ammunition and then encourage them to improve their skill so that their aim would be all the more certain in the dusk among his own stags. Just before the war I remember seeing herds of up to twenty deer each grazing on the slopes of Bleaval; I'm told that now there are none. It's a pity but, fortunately, the red deer is not an endangered species and if the Bleaval ones made the supreme sacrifice during the early war years there is some

176

comfort in the thought that they made it in the cause of peace and as a contribution to the training of our Home Guard.

I repaid my promise of ten yards of tweed many times over. The Hattersley Domestic loom had made its appearance in the Western Isles in the 1920s but the weavers of those early days were chary of change and, besides, there was a strong lobby which resisted anything that suggested a mechanisation of the old handloom weaving. Already both the warp and the weft were being spun in the mills and, by the time the war began, the spinning wheel – once a feature of every living room in Harris – was being relegated to the loft or the barn. The crofter would send his raw fleeces away to a mill with instructions regarding the colours he wanted and, in due course, he would receive back a sack of large bobbins of thread which he only had to thread into his old handloom and weave laboriously, swinging his weaver's beam with his left hand, firing his shuttle with his right, and meshing the threads of his warp by stamping on each of four sturdy wooden levers in the order demanded by his pattern. The Hattersley Domestic eliminated almost all of the back-break. The weaver set his pattern by selecting a combination of little steel plates which governed a box of six shuttles, each of which could carry a different colour of thread, and, once the loom was set up, all the weaver had to do was sit back and pedal two pedals and keep a careful eye on the warp and the weft lest a thread break. It was monotonous work but one could see the web of tweed steadily growing in front of one's eyes. In vain the older weavers protested that their tweeds were no longer hand-woven, that they were foot-woven. The war and an incredible upsurge in the demand for tweed swept aside their protests and the click-clack of the Hattersley was soon as familiar a noise as the rasp of the corncrake. The vast majority of people if asked to name the noise they associated with war would say 'gunfire'; for me it would be the chatter of the Hattersley and the twice daily drone of 'our own wee Lysander' overhead.

I don't know how many yards of tweed I would have been coaxed to contribute to the islands' annual turn-over of some three million yards in the early war years if I hadn't learnt long since that I must never be seen to be good at anything resembling physical labour. God knows it was difficult to be bad at weaving on the Hattersley when all I had to do was to sit and pedal, but I soon discovered that by altering the rhythm of the pedalling I could achieve a slackness in the weave which offended my father's pride of craftsmanship, and by failing to notice that the thread in a particular shuttle had broken, I could turn out a few yards of tweed which bore a vague resemblance to lace. There was only one way father could sort that out and that was by unravelling the tweed right back to the last correct section, re-setting the tension of the warp and starting all over again. His nerve couldn't take much of that, particularly since he couldn't be confident that the roll of tweed already woven and wrapped round the receiving roller wouldn't, when unrolled, reveal a few inches of something resembling a hairy broderie anglaise.

'For Heaven's sake keep away from that loom or my tweeds will be black-listed from John O' Groats to Lands End. Stick to your books and you might make a minister if nothing else. Meantime why don't you go down to the beach and see if anything has come ashore?'

Every coast dweller is an instinctive beachcomber, and it's a very narrow line of conscience that separates the ebb-searcher from the wrecker of the Cornish legends. Very early on in the war Old Hector's prophecy of the beach 'being covered in flotsam from end to end' came true, and whenever the tide ran with a westerly wind the Atlantic spewed up a whole assortment of stuff ranging from wooden pit-props to bales of exotic textiles. One didn't pause to think that these represented destruction – that they represented the cargoes of ships that had been torpedoed as they sought to cross the Atlantic east or west; they were the spoils of war without the immediate association of death and tragedy. Only on the very rare occasion (and the occasions were astonishingly rare considering the circumstances) when a body was washed ashore, did one really associate the spoils with the sorrow. And beachcombing became a fever, with people constantly scanning the horizon to spot a larger floating item, or else prowling the tide-line after the ebb. An official Receiver of Wrecks had been appointed to handle and report on any objects of interest or of value. And the Home Guard was given a certain amount of responsibility to contact the authorities regarding wreckage of a naval or military nature. But, in the end, it was the sharp eyed finder who decided for

178

himself whether an object on the beach was of interest to any branch of His Majesty's Government. Patently a hogshead of rum which had been contaminated by sea-water was the total responsibility of some branch of the Government and the finder would hopefully claim salvage; on the other hand, if the contents of the hogshead were unadulterated, there was no way in which any amount of petty salvage reward could compensate for the intrinsic value of the commodity itself in a community which had only one public house peddling strictly rationed beer and the occasional dram of whisky. Our villagers were so far from the nearest bar that they had never become dedicated or regular drinkers, but if Fate threw up a barrel of good quality spirits on the shore it would have taken exceptional fortitude to spurn it or turn it over to some anonymous authority. It was very rarely that that particular problem arose. The stuff which was washed up was, usually, of little interest to Customs and Excise, but it could be of great community value. A sack of flour in salt water forms an inch of thick soggy crust round the inside of the bag thus making it waterproof and protecting ninety-five percent of the contents so that they are as dry and fresh as they were the day they were milled; half-hundredweight kebbucks of butter and lard are, by their very greasy nature, waterproof anyway, and the greatest damage that they suffered was that when they rolled on the lip of the depositing wave they collected overcoats of fine sand to a depth of an inch or so. In the normal course of events one wouldn't have bothered with the gritty exterior but wartime restrictions had induced an instinct for economy even where flotsam was concerned, and the outside layers of butter and lard were fed to the cattle who would, in due course, get rid of the sand in their own way; just to be on the safe side, in case the next half inch layer had been tainted by sea water it was used to grease the loom; only the fresh pure lard or butter from the core of the lump was reserved for human consumption. The Hattersley chattered smoothly with its greasing of lard and the cattle beasts never looked glossier. The only sufferers (and only for short periods) were the local merchants who must have wondered why people didn't bother to take up their rations of butter and cooking-fat.

One day my brother and I came home with a handful of beautiful pegs, each of about six inches in length, with which we

179

proceeded to decorate the front door. Nobody paid any attention to us, at first, but by the time we had achieved a clumsy figure 7 and a crude brass knocker my father couldn't fail but notice.

'What the devil are you doing to the door, and where did you find those things?'

We explained that an old anti-shipping mine had been washed up and that we had managed to screw some of the horns off it; we would go back later with a spanner and remove the rest.

'The first thing you will do is take a hammer and remove those damn things from the door. And then, if you haven't anything better to do wind some bobbins for the Hattersley so that I can finish off that tweed when I come back!'

We thought it injudicious to ask where he was going, and it didn't matter anyway because he never got there. Half-way to the gate he stopped, spun round on his heel and came racing back.

'What did you say? An old mine? How do you know it was old?'

'If it had been a new one it would have exploded when it hit the beach, wouldn't it?'

'And if it had exploded it wouldn't be there, would it? Don't you dare go near that beach today, and if you see anybody else going in the direction of the shore stop them. I'm going to contact the Coast Guard.'

This time there was no doubt where he was going – and in a hurry. He was going to the Duchess's shop and the phone.

Early that evening a large lorry with a dozen soldiers aboard roared into the village from Stornoway. They flung open the gate to the Common Grazing and trundled towards the beach, sending sheep and cattle scattering in every direction. From the hillock above the house my brother and I watched them spilling out of the lorry. Ten of them grouped round the vehicle while two moved cautiously towards the mine which was, by now, beginning to wobble gently in the incoming tide. They seemed to take only seconds to come to a decision, and after much gesticulating from the soldier who seemed to be in charge, the main body split up and soldiers fanned out towards the village houses while the two who had examined the mine began to uncoil a huge drum of cable from the back of the lorry. In no time at all each house in the village had been visited, and the occupants warned to keep clear of their windows. A soldier was posted at each entrance to the village to stop any traffic, and then the troop moved their vehicle in behind a large sand dune and crouched down round it. When the explosion came it shook every window in the township and the reverberation of it was felt in Drumpound, two miles away.

The cows were beginning to settle down and graze again as the army lorry drew up at our gate, and a sergeant marched smartly to the door. My father invited him in and handed him the eight brass pegs which we had dutifully prized off the door.

'You screwed these off the mine?' the sergeant asked, looking from me to my brother and back to me again.

'Yes. But we didn't think we were doing any harm.'

'And then you hammered them?'

We nodded.

'Bloody hell! I don't know whether it's God or the devil looking after you, but somebody is. If that mine had gone up when you were unscrewing these horns we wouldn't have found a trouser button off one of you. And how you got away with hammering them, I'll never know. Each of them contains a detonator which would, at the very least, have taken the hands off you if one of them had decided to explode!'

He looked at my parents, both of whom were ashen-faced. I don't know what reaction he was expecting, but my mother merely forced a tight smile and said 'Would you like to bring your boys in for a cup of tea?' It was her automatic reaction to any tense situation, but it diffused this one. The sergeant laughed.

'You Lewis women! If the devil himself appeared at the door you'd offer him a cup of tea.'

'I don't know what Lewis women would do,' said my father. 'The devil might well find them more approachable than Harris women.'

'O God, I'm sorry; I'll never get it right. O.K., O.K. I'm not in Britain, I'm in Scotland. And this end of the island is Harris and the other end is Lewis. And I don't know what a poor bloody Birmingham man is doing here anyway –'

'Never you mind –' My father was warming to the idea of

181

company. 'Just bring in the lads and the wife'll put the kettle on while she's forgiving you.'

'I can't do that; there are twelve of us!'

'Yourself and eleven disciples. We know what happened to the other one. Just you go and bring them in, and we'll find enough cups to go round.'

And so, a troop of hefty Royal Engineers crowded into our tiny living room and found themselves perches somehow or other. In no time at all I could hardly see their faces for smoke as they chatted and my mother plied the teapot.

'And what's the news on the war front?' my father asked when the banter died down and the subject of the mine was thankfully exhausted. My brother and I had been mercilessly ribbed. At first we had taken it in good part, thankful that nobody was taking a more serious view of our exploit, but now the whole thing was becoming tedious and we were grateful to my father for changing the direction of the conversation.

'News?' pondered the sergeant. 'I don't know. Nothing that you won't have heard on the radio. O, there was that bit of excitement at the beginning of the week. One of those little reconnaissance planes. One of our lads heard her engine cutting out suddenly and she just disappeared. It was very misty and nobody saw anything. The Coast Guard and some fishing boats spent two days searching round the coast, and we were turned out. But nothing's been found. Poor chap – probably thought himself lucky to be on a milk run, but that's the way it goes.'

'O, no!'

My father's tone made some of the soldiers turn to look at him. There was a sad kind of smile on his face.

'It would be our own wee Lysander,' he said. 'Sure as anything. I wondered why I hadn't heard it for a few days.'

'Your own what?' the sergeant asked.

'Nothing at all. I'd just got sort of used to the sound of that wee aeroplane. It was daft, but it made one feel kind of safe to have it around.'

'That's the way it goes,' shrugged the sergeant, handing his empty cup to my mother. 'Somebody somewhere will be missing him. Just hope he's washed ashore somewhere; it's not so bad when you know for sure what happened and when you know a chap's had a decent burial.' He chattered on as he rose and put his cap on and waited for the company to get to its feet. 'Thanks for the tea, Missus. Twelve's a hell of a lot of teas out of your rations; next time there's a jeep down this way I'll get the boys to drop you off a couple of packets.'

'Not at all,' protested my mother as she followed them out to the door. 'It was a great pleasure.' Father got up but didn't say anything. I knew that he was thinking of the 'wee Lysander' which had become a strange symbol of something for him. I caught his eye as he went out after the rest, and he gave a hint of a wistful little smile. He never referred to 'our own wee Lysander' again; not even when one which looked to me identical took its place.

When the truck pulled away from the gate my brother turned to me. 'How many soldiers were in here?'

'Twelve. Why?'

'No. There were only eleven.'

'Don't be daft; the sergeant himself said twelve.'

'I know he did, but I counted eleven. And I counted twelve on the lorry when it went down to the beach. I think one of them got blown up!'

'Rubbish!' But I wasn't all that sure of myself. Donald was twelve and already beginning to show evidence of the thrawn-ness which was to serve him well in later life. I was much more inclined to accept a statement of fact without examining it, and the fact that the sergeant had said 'twelve' was enough for me. But I did know that Donald could count.

'Right then. Let's go down to the shore and have a look. Are you sure he didn't just stay behind in the lorry while the rest were having their tea?'

'No. I was trying to get into the lorry, but it was locked and there was nobody inside it.'

We slipped out to the back of the house and waited till father and mother returned from waving their unexpected guests farewell. As soon as they were indoors we set off for the beach like a couple of greyhounds out of their traps. My imagination had by now gone into top gear and I had visions of bits of flesh and khaki splattered over the rocks of the Blue Skerry.

But we weren't the first on the scene. As we reached the edge of the band of marram which separated the beach from the soft grazing we saw Gillespie waving frantically to us from the rim of

183

one of the big sandy gouges which pitted the shore-line. Gillespie and I had been closer than brothers all our lives, and had been in countless scrapes together, but he had decided not to go on to High School and had now finally left school aged fourteen. Leaving school at fourteen meant being pitched into an early manhood, and already an indefinable maturity had come down on him and a little of the laughter had gone out. That, and the physical separation when I had moved out of the village to school in the Northlands, had dropped a gossamer of reticence between us, but that was reft now by the full hurtle of Gillespie's excitement.

'Hurry up! There's a dead soldier here.' I could detect a touch of nervousness in his exuberance. 'I found him,' he added as if, even with a corpse, finders were keepers.

'I told you there were only eleven,' my brother puffed as we reached the crater.

Sure enough, there, on the bottom of the sandpit beside an electrical plunger, lay a soldier face down. We stood high above him, staring down on him like three ragged vultures, and for my own part I felt the beginnings of fear coming over me. And then the corpse muttered something and turned over on his back with a smile on his face.

'Look at him,' Gillespie spluttered. 'He's not dead at all; he's found the place where Sandy Cravat hid his rum and he's blind drunk!' Sure enough, when the man rolled over we could see that he had been lying on top of a bottle which had slipped out of his fingers and now lay on its side with a damp patch of sand at its neck. Gillespie's assessment of the situation was manifestly right. Some weeks before, Sandy Cravat had found a large cask of rum on the beach and, unlike some of the liquor that came ashore, this was unadulterated by sea water and very strong. Unfortunately the local men, who weren't very devout drinkers anyway, didn't at all fancy rum and Sandy, who used to claim that he could drink turpentine with a spoonful of sugar in it, was left with a whole cask to himself. He solved his problem in a typically Sandy way; he filled and cached forty bottles for his own immediate needs, topped the cask with water and re-bunged it. He then claimed salvage, which he got along with a letter commending him for his honesty. The whole village knew roughly where the rum was hidden but it had remained undisturbed till the sapper with a thirst stumbled on it that day.

'We'd better get him to your house; your father will know what to do with him.'

The soldier raised his head cautiously when he heard Gillespie speaking in Gaelic and then, in perfect Gaelic, asked who the hell we were. That was a bit difficult to explain; we were just ourselves – unlike him in a place where we had every right to be. So instead of telling him about us we told him about him – how his comrades had gone off without him, and how we'd found him dead drunk, and how we'd telephone Stornoway and get them to send the lorry back for him.

'O God, don't do that,' he implored with his head in his hands. 'Give me time to think. If you phone Stornoway it'll be the bloody M.P.s they'll send down and I'll be on more charges than I have fingers. I'm the odd man out in the damn platoon; I'm the only Gaelic speaker in it and that sod of an English sergeant has his knife in me.'

That put a different complexion on things. This was one of our own men – from the island of South Uist as it turned out, and in that particular regiment because he had enlisted in London. We weren't going to let any English upstart get the better of him and so we began to oxter him towards our house. My brother, with more savvy than I would have given him credit for, buried the empty rum bottle in the sand and covered over the remainder of Sandy's cache which the South Uistman had unwittingly exposed.

Father's pipe nearly fell out of his mouth when we arrived at the house with three of us supporting something which must have looked like a marionette in a uniform.

'What the devil have you got there?'

'It's a soldier.'

'You could have fooled me; but it explains a lot about the way the war's going. Where did you find him? Washed up on the beach or blown down over the hill?'

'I beg your pardon, Sir.' The hapless soldier tried to pull himself together. We had informed him that my father had been a regular soldier (which he had been, more or less) and an officer in the Home Guard (which he wasn't). 'I got separated from my platoon and –'

'He comes from South Uist and he speaks Gaelic,' I chipped in.

'That explains even more.' The stench of rum was beginning to fill the room, and my mother, sizing up the situation, had already begun bustling with the kettle. I could see laughter in my father's eyes although he was still clipped and formal. He sniffed. 'You smell to me more like a navyman. Anyway, sit down. Perhaps a cup of tea will sober you up till we decide what we're going to do with you.'

Poor Private MacAulay, as we had discovered him to be, was not, I suspected, a very articulate person at the best of times and there was something about him which suggested that he had attained the highest rank that the army would ever consider bestowing on him. So the three of us took turns to tell his story for him while he laboured over his cup of tea; we spelt out in detail the fate that would befall him when the English sergeant discovered that he was missing. The idea of an English sergeant versus a South Uist private of limited resilience had the same chauvinistic effect on my father as it had had on ourselves. One could sense him switching his mind into action.

'Finlay. Run as fast as you can move your legs and get Sandy Cravat for me. Tell him I want him here in his Home Guard uniform in five minutes flat, and if he as much as opens his mouth in protest tell him that he'd better think up a good explanation for forty bottles of rum on which he has been paid salvage money.'

I was nothing loath to give Sandy, who could be a cocky devil, his come-uppance, and by the time I had embellished my father's message he couldn't get into the uniform fast enough even although there was very definite apprehension writ large all over him. By the time we reached our house, I could hear something that sounded suspiciously like the army truck rumbling up the Back of Scarista hill.

'Good for you, Sandy.' My father's manner was positively jubilant. 'And you remembered to bring your rifle with you; we'll make a soldier of you yet.'

That was the last thing Sandy wanted; he had applied for exemption on every ground from excema to insanity, and, with the help of the local doctor he had, so far, resisted the call to the Colours. He was in the Home Guard only because somebody had told him they'd be holding regimental dances. He opened his mouth to protest or to query, but my father cut him short.

'We've no time to talk. Just remember forty bottles of illegal rum –'

'That's blackmail!'

'I know that. Powerful stuff sometimes. This is the soldier that you came across down at the Blue Skerry when you were out on patrol just about the time that they exploded the mine. From the way he was lurking in the sand dunes you thought he was a German spy and you knocked him out and locked him in the Scaristaveg barn and you waited till he came round from the terrible blow you had given him. You arrived here with him just as the army lorry was moving away, and you're here now because I told you that I was fairly certain the truck would come back.' My father heard the squeal of brakes at the gate and added, 'As it has done.'

'Bloody hell, what are you talking about. If this gets out people will think I'm mad!'

'Exactly. That's precisely what I'll tell the big sergeant who is approaching the door now. Who knows, this might get you your exemption. Just remember – you thought he was a German spy … you knocked him out … he took a long time to come round … you brought him here –' The knock on the door cut him short, and he went out to open it. He closed the living room door behind him as he went, but we could hear every word.

'Hello, Sergeant, I'm glad to see you again –'

'Sorry to bother you, Mr Macdonald, but I've lost one of my men.'

'O dear, that's sad. And his poor next-of-kin probably thinking he was safe in these parts. Ah well, that's war for you –'

The sergeant chuckled. 'No, no. I don't mean lost in that sense. I mean he's wandered off somewhere and I can't find him. I wondered if you'd seen him around?'

'O! You mean you've mislaid him. Goodness me, in my day the Colonel would have had something to say about that. I hope our landlord, Colonel Walker, doesn't hear about it; he tends to think that he's still on active service. Where do you think you left your poor man?'

'I didn't just leave him. He – er – well – I thought he was with us and then when I checked – well –' The chuckle was gone from the sergeant's voice.

'Ach, yes, Sergeant. And twelve soldiers take a lot of counting. Keep your fingers crossed that they never land you with a whole regiment. But come in, anyway, and see what we've got here for you …'

The sergeant's face was purple when he came through the living room door, but a few extra veins popped into prominence when he saw Private MacAulay drooping beside Sandy Cravat. They looked for all the world like Stan Laurel (of film comedy fame) with a taller twin brother.

'What the hell's this? Can I have an explanation, Private MacAulay?' He looked at Sandy Cravat. 'And who the devil are you?'

I could sense that my mother was getting uneasy at the kind of language with which her brood had been regaled all afternoon, but her uneasiness was sophisticated confidence compared with Private MacAulay and Sandy Cravat. My father stepped hastily into the silence.

'Let me explain, Sergeant. This is Corporal Cravat of the Home Guard. He's got his stripes but his mother hasn't had time to sew them on for him. A great soldier – you might care to make a bid for him.' Sandy Cravat looked as if he would have done something with his rifle if it had been loaded. 'But Sandy met his match in your tough Private MacAulay. You see, Corporal Cravat was on Home Guard patrol round about the time you were fiddling with the mine and didn't he go and stumble across this suspicious looking character whom he assumed, naturally, on this kind of coast, to be one of those German spies that they're putting ashore from submarines.'

'What German spies are they putting ashore from submarines? Why the hell should they – O never mind, carry on.'

My father was enjoying himself.

'And when your man started talking about blowing up something Corporal Cravat became even more suspicious, especially when he noticed that the man's accent didn't belong to any category that we're familiar with in these parts. You see, Sergeant –'

'But dammit, man, Private MacAulay speaks Gaylick and Garlick or whatever you call it!'

'Precisely. And what language would a good German spy make a point of learning if he was going to try and infiltrate a community like this? Why, Gaelic of course. And unfortunately, coming from the island of South Uist Private MacAulay's Gaelic is not the most fluent variety compared to the poetic kind that we speak in these parts.' It was Private MacAulay's turn to squirm but he was on a spit from which he couldn't descend. 'In short,' my father went on, 'Private MacAulay's Gaelic has got the sort of guttural quality which you would expect from a German student of the language. Gaelic is very poetic, you see –'

'O for God's sake. I'm very sorry, Mr Macdonald, but I have no time to go into the finer points of your native language. I don't think the war's going to last long enough for me to learn it.'

'No, perhaps not. But if you don't learn to look after your men better, and count them from time to time, it'll maybe be German that we'll all have to be learning. Now, you'll be treating Private MacAulay well, I'm sure, when you take him away. You needn't worry about any of us spreading stories about how you lost him, so long as we know he's well looked after; he may be a South Uistman but he's an islander for all that and we islanders like to look after our own.'

'I can see that,' said the sergeant with the last vestiges of his patience gone. 'Come along Private MacAulay; we'll stop on the way and telephone to make sure that somebody has your bath run and ready for you. Good-bye, Mrs Macdonald.' He managed a half smile for my mother who had been silent during the whole scene. His 'Good-bye' to my father was much crisper, and thrown over his shoulder as he marched through the door with MacAulay in dazed pursuit. Father stood at the door watching them walking down the path, and he suddenly remembered something just as the sergeant hauled himself into the passenger seat of the truck leaving MacAulay to be hauled into the back by his comrades, who made no attempt to hide their impatience. 'Sergeant, be sure that you don't ask Private MacAulay to drive; I had to force a tumbler of rum down the poor chap's throat to bring him round after the mauling Sandy gave him.'

'I'll arrange a personal chauffeur for Private MacAulay,' shouted the sergeant as he slammed the door and the truck roared off.

My father was chuckling as he came back into the living room. 'I haven't enjoyed myself so much for a long time. You know, I haven't ever met a Birmingham man with a sense of humour. Sandy, after all that I don't think we'll have any bother getting you made a sergeant in the Home Guard. The more that man tells his story the better you'll come out of it, and once you're a sergeant in the Home Guard they'll have you into the real army in no time.'

'Bloody hell, I don't want to go into the real army. How often do I have to tell you? I don't want to be a hero. I want to stay at home here and look after my parents and run the croft. If you could get me kicked out of the Home Guard it would be the greatest favour you could do me.'

Father sat down on St Clement's bench and began to fill his pipe. 'Well, we might find a way to do that too – you never know. If you were to go and dig up a bottle of that rum of yours it might help us think.'

'Haven't you done enough blackmailing for a day, without putting the screws on me for a bottle of rum which I'd give you anyway, just for the polite asking.'

'You and your blackmail, Sandy. It's people like you who give blackmail a bad name; there's nothing wrong with it when it's used moderately and in a good cause.'

Sandy shuffled off muttering something about people who would sit happily on the right side of the law watching others doing their dirty work for them. He had a point. Nobody had lifted a finger to help him with the cask of rum (had it been whisky it would have been a different matter) but whenever the mood took somebody poor Sandy was sent off to dig up another of his bottles with the threat of exposure always hanging over his head. Just as Sandy arrived back with his bottle of rum Tom-of-the-Oaths and the Man with the hole in his cheek strolled up to the door as if on cue. They had come to discuss some township business but whatever it was got pushed further and further down the agenda as drams were poured from Sandy's bottle and father gave a highly embroidered account of Private MacAulay's adventures. From being non-existent

Sandy Cravat's role in the affair became more and more heroic, and the more he protested the more the newcomers were disposed to believe my father's invention. By the time the bottle was finished they were at the stage of discussing a letter to General Lang recommending Sandy for a commission in the Cameron Highlanders.

'Do that and I'll put a bullet through my foot the next time we're on Home Guard parade, and that'll make sure I'll fail the medical. That's how much I want to go into the bloody army!'

The Man with the hole in his cheek looked horrified.

'You'd do that!' he said. 'And you with your Home Guard boots on. They're the King's boots man. Nobody's going to worry about your foot, but if they hear that you're threatening to damage Government property even before you're in the army they'll have you on Court Martial even before you're in uniform!'

It was an evening which, in its cosiness, reminded me of our early years in the new house in the new village. There was laughter and teasing just as there had been then although the themes were different. For a brief while the gap which had been developing between me and the village had disappeared. These were my people – the people who had moulded my youth more than the school-teachers of the Southlands or the Northlands. What mattered it if the Northlands had shops, and Big Grandfather's house had a bathroom instead our 'end of the house' or 'outside'. Here was the warmth. And suddenly, out there in the dusk, a corncrake rasped a note of scorn as if she were saying, 'We'll see if the mood of the balmy evening will last through the chill of the dawn.' Sandy Cravat must have noticed a jerk in my mood; up to that point I'd been silent on the fringe of the banter.

'For God's sake Finlay, see and do well in that school of yours. Make sure you get to Portree, if only to get yourself away from this mob; they tell me if you go in for the kirk you're exempt from the army.'

Sandy's remark was a re-statement of the corncrake's fancied comment and it brought me back to reality with a thud. I was only at the beginning of my long road on which Tarbert school was only a milestone. Success in Tarbert meant that I would go on to a higher grade school in Portree in Skye. Success in

191

Portree would mean that I would go on to University in one of the cities. Success in University would mean that I would be unlikely to return to the community again since our community offered little scope for men with degrees. In short, success meant that this was one of the last evenings that I would spend in the village ...

It was late when the men went away in great good form. The rum had mellowed everybody and even Sandy Cravat's equanimity had returned as the veterans assured him that not even an English regiment would look at him. Father was smiling to himself as he checked the dying embers before dousing the lamp. Then, in the stillness, there came the distant sound of an aeroplane and he paused and looked as if he were going to say something. But he shrugged and carried on with his chore.

I was dropping off to sleep when a thunderous knocking came to the door. I swung my feet off my make-shift bed and I could hear father thumping to the floor in the bedroom. 'Who is it?' he shouted.

'Don't worry,' said the familiar voice of the Boer War veteran. 'It's only myself. There's nothing wrong. It's just an air-raid warning and the rules say that I've got to let you know. Just go back to sleep. I'll waken you later with the All-clear.'

But he didn't. Not that night or the night after, nor on any of the nights that remained to me in the village before I set off again on that long road into the future. Perhaps, like myself, the Boer War veteran assumed that peace would reign in the village anyway whether an official All-clear was announced or not.